Lorraine's Journey of Faith

Lorraine P. Woodhouse
with Maria A. Deed

Lorraine's Journey of Faith

*Life is a journey that can only
be lived through faith*

Lorraine P. Woodhouse
with Maria A. Deed

Published by Lorraine P. Woodhouse

Lakewood, CA, U.S.A.

Printed in the U.S.A.

Edited by Dominique Leola Deed

Cover Design: HeyerVision.com

© 2018 Lorraine P. Woodhouse with Maria A. Deed Lorraine's Journey of Faith

ISBN -13 978-0-692-10653-2

For additional information please e-mail

zech4_6@icloud.com

Contents

INTRODUCTION

I was encouraged by friends, after I had shared some experiences that God was doing in my life during my stand for my marriage, to write a book. I did not want to accept that, as I was in no way able to write a book; but after a few more encouraging words, the Holy Spirit began to work on me concerning these suggestions. It was always at night when I got into bed that the Holy Spirit would bring all these things that had taken place during my stand: discipline, the changes He wanted to make in my life, guidance, prayer, and obedience to Him. This took place on many nights for about a year.

I just could not see myself writing a book. Sometimes I would grab a pen and jot things down, but I would feel it was impossible and would go back to bed. This frustrated me so much, and I struggled and struggled with this idea. One day in prayer I asked the Lord why He always initiated these thoughts when I wanted to sleep. His answer was that during the day I was so involved in my activities that I couldn't hear Him! He asked, "Do you want to keep it a secret, all that I have done in your life and for you?" What could I say other than, "Of course not!" But a book?

Then I was asked to give my testimony at C. K. conference and that was sort of the way God began leading me toward this book. I began to pray for help in bringing this about. God sent the help, in a strange way! I needed some help on my computer and I was told that a lady who worked at the church could help me with that. Well, as Maria Deed helped me several times with my computer, I started to share with her about this book God was urging me to write, and she offered her help. God's leading again.

So, we began with recording and dictation. It really was a challenge and I wasn't sure if this could ever be possible, but we began with prayer each time. This took several months, and then finally it was ready for editing. My hope and prayer for this book is that it will encourage others, that God will use it to direct or change a life, and that it will bring His victory and glory in a life and marriage just as He did for me.

ACKNOWLEDGMENTS

I want to thank so many for the input, encouragement, advice and counsel I received, starting with Pastor Dr. Borror from Lakewood Baptist Church. Also, Pastor Jeff Johnson from Calvary Chapel Downey for all of the sermon tapes that I collected and was able to listen to over and over. Louise Riffle, truly the mentor God provided me, with helping, encouraging and strongly advising me. Vickie Southerland, my assistant prayer advisor from the Ministry of Christian Women's club, was sent by God for support. I truly thank God for bringing these two dedicated ladies into my life, who are also my friends.

Thank you to the Covenant Keepers Inc. ministry, which became a significant influence for my stand: to the leaders of the ministry who have guided so many with troubled marriages. God is building hope and healing for all who have decided to go God's way for marriage. To those in this ministry, I offer my thanks and praise to God. To Marilyn Conrad, founder of C. K., and to the leaders of group meetings I attended. Also, to the new leaders, Rex and Carolyn Johnson, who took over after Marylin stepped down. What a blessing this ministry is! I was privileged to meet so many wonderful friends and we were all an encouragement to one another. We are an army against divorce. Thank you to Gloria Jackson, who took a stand for her marriage and sent me many articles that enhanced my faith as well. When you ask God for help, He will lead and supply.

A big thank-you to Maria and Dominique, who were so instrumental in providing the time and help to produce this book.

Rebecca Lawson, Jennifer Cullis, and Robert Heyer thank you for the endless help you provided, may God bless each one of you!

God is so faithful to guide our lives while He challenges us in His own ways. To Him go all the praise and the glory and the honor.

Journal Entry

November 12, 1980

*L*orraine, I want you to read this every morning: "You have trusted Me in a few things and I have not failed you, My child. Trust Me now for everything and see if I will not do for you immeasurably more than you could ever ask or think. Not according to your power, your faith, your prayers or your ability, Lorraine, but according to My mighty power that is within."

Lord, I'm learning, and this is for Your plan, not for mine. I turn it over to You.

You don't find it difficult to trust Me with the management of the universe, do you? Can your situation be so complex that you need to be anxious about how I manage your marriage, your husband, and or you?

No, Lord. I serve a loving God who cares, I know.

So get those thoughts out of your mind. Don't let them linger. Take your stand on the power and trustworthiness of Me, your God! And see how quickly all the doubts and fears will vanish. They are the culprits that bring all the evil thoughts, distress, depression, and discouragement. Self-pity and jealousy are sins that we must repent of. Loneliness and the desire to give up cause a dark cloud to hover over you. I don't want that for you, My child. If your eyes are on Me, all these will vanish and will be replaced by a steadfast determination to believe in Me and My power.

Trust Me in the dark, Lorraine, when you don't see and you don't hear what is going on or you don't receive the encouragement that you want from Howard. Don't look to Howard. Look to Me and remember.

Yes, Lord.

Trust Me in the light, in the night, and in the morning. This may require some work at first and a lot of effort at times but sooner or later it will just become natural and habitual. You know this so well, My child, but it bears repeating to you. You have the words of Jesus reminding you:

Looking at them, Jesus said, "With people it is impossible, but not with God; for all things are possible with God." (Mark 10:27)

And what more shall I say? For time will fail me if I tell of Gideon, Barak, Samson, Jephthah, of David and Samuel and the prophets, who by faith conquered kingdoms, performed acts of righteousness, obtained promises, shut the mouths of lions, quenched the power of fire, escaped the edge of the sword, from weakness were made strong, became mighty in war, put foreign armies to flight. (Hebrews 11:32-34)

Faith can do it again, My child. Don't be concerned about how much faith you have or don't have, for I have dealt to a man a measure of faith and that faith is in you. Just let the faith take over your thoughts and actions. You have spoken to your mountain, according to Matthew 17:20; now praise me that it is done, and just keep telling yourself, "I can trust my God and I will trust Him. For all the powers of hell shall not be able to make me doubt God's Word, His promises, and the faithfulness of my redeemer." Remember, I need and want your trust in Me, and nothing is so sweet to Me as such total, reckless trust. And let not condemnation and guilt send dark clouds over you, My child, for you are special in My sight. I love you. Let your faith confirm all My promises to you. My child, I have given you many, many promises, so believe. I will see you through and I will come through for you.

Do not harden your hearts, as at Meribah, As in the day of Massah in the wilderness. (Psalm 95:8)

These trials and attacks will come, but let your faith prove itself worthy of all praise, glory and honor when I, Jesus Christ, reveal the victory. Look up and keep looking up. Take hold now, My child. I have not failed you and I will not fail you or forsake you. Resist the devil and his accusations and all the thoughts, imaginations and attitudes that he tries to put in your mind. Look at My promises. You are Mine. You are My child. I will perfect all that concerns you.

That's why you need My help and My divine companionship. I do not fail to give you the right help and to understand your need and struggle as only I can. Life is not easy, My child, for man has not made of it what My Father meant it to be. I have made straight paths for My children to follow, but they have made it devious, evil, filled with obstacles and stones of difficulty. I realize this is not an easy task I have set before you. I am asking you to walk in the way of obedience. It's to love through Me in the impossible way and not to love in the human realm, for that is impossible. Howard has accepted Me in his life but has not yet made Me Lord of his life. Your prayers for him will be reached only by the spirit of love. Love is the only magnet that will draw him and others to Me. Be true, be strong, be loving.

God, I can't do this on the human level. I need Jesus' love to flow through me.

Yes, I realize that Howard is opposing you right now, that he may disregard much that you consider of value, and that he may not want to receive your love and help. His aims may seem unworthy to you and his self-seeking antagonizes you, but My command says, "Judge not, My child." Can you limit My words to suit your own inclinations?

Lord, I receive Your chastisement and Your discipline for my life, even though it hurts a little or a lot at times.

My child, by My spirit you have miracle-working power in action today as it once was years ago. Whenever you trust wholly in me and cleave to me, the choosing of the very day and hour, My miracle-working power will be manifest as marvelously today as it was when I was on Earth. As ever it was to set free, work miracles of wonder and bring healing, both spiritually and physically. Trust in me, My child. Release your boundless faith and you will see, and seeing will give Me all the glory.

See your marriage healed before it is totally manifested. I will see the restoration in My spirit. Remember and say often to yourself, "Not by might, nor by power, but by My Spirit sayeth the Lord." I, your Lord, your friend, can accomplish this now in your life and apply these miracles to your present-day need. Your husband has return and your marriage has healed; know that your help and salvation are sure. Remember, My child:

Again I say to you, that if two of you agree on earth about anything that they may ask, it shall be done for them by My Father who is in heaven. (Matthew 18:19)

There are many praying and I am in the midst of all those prayers. Claim this promise always, and think what this means in power. It is again the lesson of the power that follows two united in prayer. I am the truth if two shall agree; every word of Mine is true. Every promise of Mine shall be fulfilled.

I will lift up my eyes to the mountains; From where shall my help come? My help comes from the LORD, Who made heaven and earth. (Psalm 121:1-2)

I know you become weary at times but remember that I bring rest also for the weary; this weariness must compel you to rest in My love. Let My love so permeate your being that you are supported by and so strengthened by it. Don't be concerned about doing a lot of things right now; just remain inactive, conscious of My presence with you. Yours is a big work, and you need to rest in My love. At this time, I choose to speak to you so that the emotional stress and activity on the physical plane do not defeat My purpose and My ends in your circumstances. I have called you aside to speak to you. I am teaching you love, obedience, and truth. Tune out all of yourself that would rebel against My ways. Check all your actions and motives that result from habit and that would be moved by self-esteem or self-pity, loneliness, jealousy, etc. Discipline yourself rather than let self gain any ascendancy; oust those rebellious acts and follow Me.

Oh, Father, please forgive those times I yielded to that self-esteem and self-pity and questioned Howard. I am sorry for the lack of discipline I have in my life at times. Help me to have better control. Thank You that my mistakes are covered by the blood of Jesus until I can reach maturity in this area. God reminded me to wait for His orders and commands, to wait for His guidance and His supply. And when I don't know what to say when a question arises or an action occurs that I'm not sure of, I can call on Him: "Quick, God; what do I say or do?"

I'm right at your side, available to help.

I sought the LORD, and He answered me, And delivered me from all my fears. (Psalm 34:4)

But you must wait on Me. Many times you came into My presence, My child, but you didn't wait for the calmness and strength that contact with Me would give you. Look unto Me and be saved, but not with a hurried glance. Look unto My face as the lover beholding the beloved; wait on Me. Wait until My strength has filled your being; leave Me to explain what I will of you and your actions. When you long for your prayers to be answered, when your need is great and you ask great things, then your way is clear. Your hope is in Me, your Lord.

Take the next simple duty that lies in your hand and seek to do that thoroughly, and so with the next; and as you do, remember My promise to you. More and more set your hopes on Me; leave your future in My hands, knowing that it will hold more and more of Me. Walk in my way, Lorraine. My way is that of doing, not only of accepting, My will; but submitting to that will, however gladly you may do so, is not enough. I need complete obedience. Your work and influence for Me will be hindered if there is no obedience. By the obedience of one, they shall be made righteous.

God, show me if I have been disobedient in any way.

Where would your salvation have been had I faltered and wavered in My task? It was by the obedience of My earthly life that I saved, and so must it be with you for Howard. Many are watching you and your circumstances in your marriage. The path that has been tried, every step has been planned with a view to your progress. This joy may come not as the reward of activity, My child. It may be the reward of patient suffering, bravely born. So trust, so conquer, and so enjoy.

Love covers the way. Love takes the sting out of the adversity. Love, love, love of Me will fill you with love for Howard. Suffer to stand, though you may not see it; but the power of victory performed by substitution sacrifice is redemptive beyond man's power of understanding here on Earth. Your future is not your concern; it is Mine. Your past you have handed back to me, and you have no need to dwell on it any longer. Do not dwell on past sorrows, resentments, and failures, or the anxieties of this day or the days ahead of you. You have the eternal God as your refuge, as Deuteronomy 33:27 reminds you—a place to flee to; a sanctuary; an escape from misunderstanding yourself, your sense of failure, your weakness, your sins, and your shortcomings to the eternal God, your refuge. Feel the relief of safety merge into a joy of appreciation, of refuge; absorb the divine, and by strength conquer. I am beside you, a very human Jesus, who understands all your weaknesses and sees too your struggles and conquests. So, fainting and needy, reach out to others and know that I will supply your need, not grudgingly, but in full measure. Draw nigh in silent awe and adoration. Draw nigh as Moses drew near to the burning bush. I gave you the loving intimacy of a friend, but I am God too; and the wonder of our relationship, the miracle of your intimacy with Me, will mean more to you if sometimes you see the majestic figure of the Son of God.

Oh, Father, I would love to see that.

1

Beginnings

God's Sovereignty

I became a Christian at twelve years of age. It all started when my dad decided to send me to a Christian youth summer camp. I did not want to go because it was sixty miles from home and I did not want to be far away from home. When we got there, I got very homesick and cried all night. Alice, the counselor in our cabin, was the youth leader at our country church. She sat on the side of my bed and tried to console me, but I just continued to cry and eventually became very sick. The next day, due to my stomach being very upset, I did not participate in any events or even go to mealtime. My counselor was very kind and she would check in on me periodically, trying to console me in love.

In the evening they had an evangelistic service that Alice finally convinced me to attend. She said that if I went with her, it would be good for me. I don't remember exactly who the speaker was or even the content of his message, but I know it touched my heart. The speaker then finished his message and gave an invitation to come forward and receive Jesus. I felt a tug at my heart; I wanted to, but I was afraid to go up myself. I then opened my eyes to see if anyone else was going; just then Alice put her hand on my shoulder. That one gesture of love just seemed to give me the courage I needed to go up—and I did. I prayed that night to accept Jesus into my life, and not only was I able to sleep through the night but I was also able to join in all the activities the next few days that we were there. I don't know why, but I don't recall sharing with my parents when I got back that I had accepted Jesus into my life.

The following year in February, my mother passed away suddenly and I became very angry at God. After all, I had just accepted Him in my life and I blamed God. I had a very hard time for several months in accepting her death. I was fighting it. I know it was very hard on my dad. My dad was a good father but I know my hurt didn't help the pain he was going through. I didn't want to accept my mother's death. Some of my family members got very angry with me. I tried so hard not to have these feelings; and as time went on, I guess I just accepted it.

I had to repeat the eighth grade because I couldn't get control of my emotions. When I started high school in the ninth grade, my dad sent me to another little town where my older sister had a beauty shop so that I could stay with her and go to school. The next year, when my younger sister started high school, he sent us both to Watertown and to a larger school about 30 miles from home. We each stayed with different families and there worked for our room and board. We didn't like it at all and begged our dad to let us come home. He told us to stay at least the first semester of school and then he would bring us home; later on he did and we were so glad to be home. We attended the same school in Hazel where my other two older sisters and brother attended and graduated from. We would catch a bus every morning; it was only four miles to that small town. The last part of that year there were only three students in my tenth-grade class: my cousin, another girl, and me.

Starting my eleventh grade, the other girl did not return but Howard joined me and my cousin. Before the end of that year, he pursued me and we would sit together on the bus to attend the basketball games. He was one of the good players on the team and I was a cheerleader. I think we had one date before the end of that year and I ended up never seeing him all summer. When we returned for our senior year, we took up our relationship again. The players and the cheerleaders would still have to take the bus to the games together and we would continue to sit together. Once in a while, his dad would let him have the car and he would bring me home from school.

We then began our courtship. When we graduated from high school, I went to work in Watertown, South Dakota, and Howard got a job in Sioux City, Iowa. We corresponded through letters. One day his father got really sick and Howard was called home to help with the farming. His father ended up passing away when Howard was 19 years old, so he had to do the farming and help out with his two younger twin brothers and a little sister.

I invited Howard to our youth groups, and every time he would come. We had an Evangelist come to our little country church for meetings and I invited Howard to come, not really sure where he was with the Lord. He had been confirmed as a Lutheran; and although I did not say it to him, I wanted to know he was saved. The night he came with me to church, he went forward and accepted Jesus into his life. In 1949 he gave me an engagement ring.

2

Family

God's Gifts

On one very cold day after I got off from work, Howard picked me up to bring me out to his place for his mother's birthday. When we got ready to leave to take me back to town, his mother told him to put his overcoat on. He didn't think he needed it but he put it on at her request. It was kind of late when we left and we had 30 miles to Watertown where I worked. After he dropped me off, on his way home, he fell asleep at the wheel and ran into a bridge abutment. When he came to, his leg was badly broken, his face was cut and bleeding, and he had to crawl up a little hill to a farmhouse for help in 10-degrees-below-zero weather. While this was happening, our youth leader was awakened at about midnight by the Holy Spirit that someone was in trouble. She didn't know who but she began to pray. She kept on praying until she felt a release and this probably was about the time Howard arrived at this home and help was on its way.

He was confined to a bed for several months. I would visit him on weekends when I would go back home; he looked forward to those weekends. By September, he was able to get around with crutches, so we decided to set our wedding date for September 17, 1950.

That evening came, and he decided to put aside his crutches. He said he wasn't going to walk down the aisle with them. He actually did very well.

We moved onto my dad's farm for a few months, until Dad decided to come back to the farm. We moved into my dad's small trailer. What little furniture we had we put in storage and lived in that small trailer until

we could find a farm to move into on our own. During this time, I became pregnant. Our son, Galen, was born October 15, 1951. When I came home from the hospital, we moved onto the farm we were renting. For three years we farmed quite a bit of land. Because we couldn't afford to hire help, I had to go out in the field to help Howard, even though he was the one to put in the long hours. He fixed an apple box with rope through holes in each end and fastened it under the tractor seat. We put Galen in that and he'd ride with his dad back and forth in the field while I would be working in another field covering the ground that Howard had just planted. When dinner time would come, 12:00 p.m., I would stop and pick up Galen, take him home, clean him up, and feed him, then put him down for a nap, which he didn't like too much. I'd make dinner for Howard and me, and after dinner we would go back out to the field. As soon as Galen would awaken, back out to the field I would go till it was time for me to go home and make supper. Farming kept us very busy as Howard would put in long hours putting in the crops. I would take care of the chores at home, feed the chickens, gather the eggs, and prepare them for the truck pick-up.

The first two years the weather was so cold that our crops didn't amount to much. It was too dry and there was no rain the first two years, and then by the third year we were hailed out completely. That's when we decided to quit farming. Howard had a cousin in California, as did I, and we corresponded by mail on and off. She urged us to visit, promising that we would love California. She was sure Howard would be able to find work. We were excited about trying that, as farming was starting to be very discouraging. I had prayed, "God, if we could be in a better place," and then did not think about it anymore. We placed our furniture in storage and our machinery we stored on my dad's farm and we left for California.

The day after we arrived at my cousin's place in California, her husband got Howard a job in the floor factory. We were really excited we had money in our pockets, and we finally got our own place in Long Beach. We were very happy. Of course, Howard didn't care for factory work because he was an outdoor boy but eventually he got a job working for a construction company, driving a water truck where construction was taking place. There was a lot of building going on in California but it was kind of seasonal work.

We took trips back to South Dakota every year to visit our families. We missed them a lot, but we were happy to have a good job we could depend on. The trips were brief since at first Howard would get only two weeks' vacation. We would drive day and night to get there so that we'd have a little more time with family. Then day and night we'd drive to get home, but we enjoyed it. As Howard's vacations increased, we would take some sightseeing trips on our way back, like through Colorado, Yellowstone, Grand Canyon, Bryce Canyon, etc. We enjoyed our family vacations. One time we just took a vacation on our own and went through Seattle, Washington, and visited some friends there, then we went across to Canada and came back down through Montana and Idaho. We stopped there and Galen and Howard did a little fishing—memories we will never forget. We also started to go on a lot of camping trips to the mountains and deserts with friends.

We soon began to feel we needed to find a home church, so we looked around for a denomination similar to the one we had been attending in South Dakota and we found a church in Anaheim. The church was quite a way from Long Beach where we were living at the time, but we went anyway. Later we found out that there was another location in Long Beach, so we started attending this church all while we moved from Long Beach to Bellflower. While we lived there I became pregnant again and, nine months later, just before Debbie was born, we ended up moving to Lakewood, where we rented a house. A neighbor across the street worked for a food industry called Thrifty Mart. He told Howard they were hiring truckers and that he should put an application in. He did it and not only did he get the job but he ended up working there for 42 years. He really enjoyed that job because he wasn't tied up in a building and it was outdoors moving around. While he worked, I stayed at home and took care of the home and our children. After we moved to Lakewood, we bought our present home, two doors from where we were renting. After the children were both enrolled in school, I took a job in a school cafeteria.

We later got involved with high school and junior high school youth groups and had many get-togethers at our house. I attended a women's Bible study group that was outside of our church for a couple years called Bible Study Fellowship. When I finished a couple years later, I was involved with Christian Women's Club of Long Beach and I was on the board. It was during this time that I began to desire a closer walk with God; so many of the speakers had just planted that desire in me because their testimonies were always so touching. I really enjoyed those meetings once a month. Their stories would just touch my heart and spirit, but I didn't know how to share that with my family. I came across in a wrong way at times, so I had to pretty much keep it all to myself.

We had a young man named Al come to our church to work with the youth. Al was involved with Youth for Christ Ministry in Long Beach. He and our son, Galen, became very close. When Galen was in high school, he became interested in the Youth for Christ Ministry and Al encouraged him when they had activities to get involved. We attended their fundraising banquets. We were excited to see how God was working with the youth.

After Galen graduated from high school, he attended City College for a couple years. He then went on to CSU LA to get his bachelor's degree in Business Administration.

Debbie graduated from high school and attended City College of Long Beach for one year without really knowing what she wanted to major in. She got a job for a while until she met someone who was going to Biola University and she decided that's where she wanted to go. Debbie took voice lessons while at our church from our choir director and developed a strong singing voice, so at Biola she joined a sextet. They would go to various churches for concerts. They were very good. We would attend as much as we could.

After Galen graduated from CSU LA with his bachelor's degree, he decided to go into full-time work with Youth for Christ. He had to raise his support and then he was sent to New Jersey for training for a year. Howard wasn't really happy about that, especially because Galen had to raise his own support, but he never made an issue about it. We went to visit Galen while he was in New Jersey and were happy in all that he was doing. He then returned to California to begin work with the ministry here in Long

Beach. He only was with them a couple months when the Board of Directors decided they just couldn't hire him due to lack of finances. Galen was so disappointed and didn't know what he should do. He talked to me about it and wondered if he should just go out and find a secular job. We should have sat down as a family and discussed the situation, but we didn't. A letter arrived at the Long Beach location from the Youth for Christ office in Indiana asking if Galen would come back and work for the ministry there. Galen felt that this was God's opening for him, but we also never discussed this as a family. Galen packed up his things, rented a U-Haul trailer, and left for Indianapolis, which just about broke Howard's heart. He just sobbed when Galen left. Needless to say, our lives began to change.

Galen's decision to pursue a ministry with Youth for Christ seemed to be the weapon Satan used to bring havoc into our home and family since we were not really grounded in the Word of God. Because we couldn't communicate our feelings to each other as a family and had no knowledge of God's Word, we were the victims of the attacks upon our lives. I was happy to see our son going into ministry but I knew that Howard was not pleased that Galen had to raise his own support. Though he didn't say it, I believe in my heart that since Galen had gotten a bachelor's degree in college, Howard had it in his mind that Galen could find a good-paying job, something Howard hadn't had a chance to do himself because he was helping his mother and family when his father passed away. He would have liked the opportunity to go to college himself. He was proud of Galen's accomplishment but he and I were not happy about Galen leaving California. We thought he was going to work for the ministry here in Long Beach, California. Unfortunately, we were looking at all of this from a worldly view and it started to turn Howard's mind.

When Galen left, we were urged by friends from our former church to visit the church they had decided to move to. I knew this was God's leading also, as He knows the road ahead of us. So, we visited this church. It was a Baptist church, which was quite different in some ways from where we came from. We were amazed at the messages we were hearing as they were unlike what we had been used to hearing; these messages were Bible-oriented. We loved the people of our church, and we loved our pastor, but we were not growing in the Lord; so the word came on strong to us through a pastor, Pastor Borror. We then decided to join this church, and Howard, Debbie and I were later baptized in this church. Howard seemed to enjoy the church but he never got involved with activities in the church except the Sunday school class and church.

He began putting in long hours at work. We were very close to our friends who had encouraged us to come and visit this church. But I knew something was bothering Howard, but he just couldn't bring himself to talk about it.

All of Howard's family—his twin brothers, his mother, his two sisters, and their families—moved to California. I also had members from my family move to California, so we now had family out here. Both the twins came out before they were married; one married out here and the other one went back to South Dakota and married my niece. They were married in South Dakota and returned to California to make their home out here.

In 1975, we celebrated our 25th wedding anniversary and flew to Hawaii. We had a good time but I noticed that Howard did not seem like himself. When we returned home, our daughter had an open house for us with family and friends. That same year Howard started working more hours and seemed to be pulling away from his relationship with God.

3

Turmoil

God's Grace

It was Thanksgiving 1976 and we had been planning to camp in the desert, a beautiful campground in Anza-Borrego, with several members from our church. We rented a little trailer house to pull behind our car. Debbie and I got the things we needed to put in the trailer for our camping trip, but when Howard came home from work he informed me that morning, as we were getting ready to leave, that he would not be able to get the entire time off. He would have to return home the evening of Thanksgiving and work Friday and Saturday. I questioned him about it since he always was able to get Thursday through Sunday off. But his answer was rather sharp to me: "Well, I just got to work!" When it came time for him to leave, I was uneasy; but I knew Howard had strange hours as a trucker, so I somewhat just accepted it. He joined us again late Saturday evening but I knew something was wrong as he was very cold to me and unresponsive. He joined in the fellowship around the campfire with everyone but he just wasn't himself. When we left to come home, I felt the chill of something very wrong as he was very quiet and distant to Debbie and me. From that time on, I just didn't know what was bothering Howard. Anytime I tried to ask him, he would get upset with me and say, "Why do you think that something is wrong?! I'm tired." So, I would drop the subject.

Then in December, we had a Sunday school Christmas party on Friday evening. A week and a half before Christmas, Howard called me late in the afternoon and told me he would not get home for the Christmas party and that I should go ahead and go. I asked what was wrong and he said, "I don't know. I just need to find myself. And I don't know when I will be home." I hung up the phone and just cried. I couldn't imagine what was wrong. Howard didn't come home until after Christmas. Unfortunately, Debbie was also away over Christmas. I cried out to God, "What is happening to our family?" When Howard came in the door, I ran up to him to give him a hug but he just brushed me away. I had made a small turkey and all the trimmings as if my family was home. I cried the whole time I was making it. Howard ate a turkey sandwich and then went into the living room and sat down in the rocking chair. I sat on his lap and told him I missed him and that I loved him. He said, "I don't know how to tell you this but I've got to let you know. I have someone else and I don't love you anymore." I was dumbfounded; that had never entered my mind. I asked him a couple of questions and he just broke down and cried and admitted to his adultery. I didn't know what to tell him. But I know that the Lord certainly helped me there, because I said, "I forgive you, honey," and that really upset him. The torture began. I got him to get up off of the floor and onto the couch and I covered him up. I tried to console him but he just wanted me to leave him alone. I went into the family room and just paced the floor and cried. I pleaded with God: "What have I done? What have I done? Whatever it is, Lord, please forgive me." As I approached the glass doors, I saw the moon shining really brightly and saw a form of a cross over the moon, and I heard, "Lorraine, I died for all of those sins and all are forgiven. Trust Me." I just fell to the floor like a dishrag, yet I felt His comfort in all my pain. Howard slept on the couch that night and I just cried myself to sleep. The next morning, he and Debbie left for work as usual.

Debbie was very disturbed and stayed away as much as she could. I felt like I was in another world, that this just couldn't be happening to us. A few days later, as Debbie was getting ready for work, she informed me that she was in love with a married man she was seeing at work. I told her not to get involved with a married man: "If he cannot be true to his wife, how can you trust him to be true to you?" She didn't accept that advice. She had an opportunity later to go to her dad and told him of the relationship. Since he was under the influence of the enemy, he gave her bad advice. His response to her was to "do whatever you want. I have someone else also." That really shocked Debbie but it gave her the opportunity to feel it was okay. Needless to say, that sent Debbie down the wrong path. Many years later, she shared with me that she had wanted a different response from her dad and had been shocked and confused at his counsel, that it had deeply affected her life. However, Debbie felt afraid of all that was going on and didn't want to face the situation we were in. Galen was in Indiana at that time so she had no one to confide in. One morning as she was getting ready for work, without looking at me she said, "I am moving out also, Mom," and she moved in with this man.

That sent me railing and crying and I called my sister. I had not been able to sleep or eat for weeks and had lost a lot of weight. I had no idea where my life was going. My sister came up and I did not even want to get out of bed. After a bit, family members decided I needed to see a doctor. I did not want to go but they insisted and I ended up in the hospital. The doctors told them I was on the verge of a nervous breakdown. I did not remain in the hospital long, as I understood that they wouldn't release me until I was able to eat. To get out of the hospital, I forced myself to eat a little more each day. When I was released I was put on valium. I took that for some time because it seemed to relieve my pain, but I really felt like I did not want to live anymore. A friend from Christian Women's Club encouraged me to go to her house so that she could fix my hair. While I was under the dryer, I was reading the Bible and God spoke to me in these verses:

Will You perform wonders for the dead? Will the departed spirits rise and praise You? Selah. Will Your lovingkindness be declared in the grave, Your faithfulness in Abaddon? Will Your wonders be made known in the darkness? And Your righteousness in the land of forgetfulness? (Psalm 88:10-12)

I began to plea: "Oh Lord, I plead for my life and will keep on pleading day by day, oh Jehovah. Why have You thrown my life away? Why are You turning Your face from me and looking the other way?" God said to me, "Lorraine, how then can you see My miracles in the grave? Will you not proclaim My faithfulness?" While in the hospital, I had been visited by one of the truckers' wives I had met through a Bible study we had attended in their home. She brought me the book The Calvary Road. She had written in it, "Lorraine, who is most important in your life? Is Christ supreme? I will be praying for you." When I got home, I glanced at the pages of this book but it only made me feel worse; it was too hard to read at the time.

I finally asked Howard if I could make an appointment with Dr. Borror and if he would agree to go with me; he said yes. He would go but he stated, "It's a little too late." Regardless, I made the appointment and we went. Dr. Borror understood that there was much conflict in our marriage, although Howard never mentioned the other woman. I listened to Howard, to his complaints that I never loved his family and that I was not a wife to him, but I never said anything. I didn't know what to say. I guess I knew I had failed somehow. Dr. Borror looked at me and asked if that was true. I answered by telling him I just didn't like the lifestyle of his family; they were not living Christian principles. Howard agreed that he did not like that either but now that was being used against me. In fact, his mother suggested we live together for a while before getting married, but I took offense to her and even though I knew it was wrong I held some bad feelings toward her. Dr. Borror asked Howard if he had tried to understand my feelings but Howard couldn't answer him. He gave us some very good scriptural advice but Howard was not ready to accept that. He then told us to go and get some counseling from another counselor so that we could get some help. He sent us to another counselor, supposedly a Christian counselor. The new counselor listened to all of Howard's complaints. He then looked at me, but I did not have much to say as I felt guilty about some of the things that Howard was telling. Then he looked at both of us and said, "I see no hope for this marriage. I advise you to get a divorce." I was shattered and we were silent on our way home. I tried to plead with Howard, but to no avail.

One day, I called Dr. Borror and made an appointment with him. I told him that I knew I had failed in many ways as a wife but was willing to let God do what He wanted to do in my life to help me. His advice was, "Lorraine, I will not counsel divorce because I believe that God hates divorce. My council to you is to seek the Holy Spirit and let Him guide you. God is the God of the impossible." He then asked me to get a book called Second Chance and to read it. He said it was a story about a troubled marriage and the wife he had counseled to stand for her marriage. I immediately got the book and began reading it. She revealed her struggle with obeying the Word concerning her role as a wife, which encouraged me. I learned that through her struggle, her obedience to God is what not only brought their marriage back together but also healed it.

Howard kept coming and going, and because of that I would just dread when Wednesday would come around. I would look forward to Sunday when he would come home again. Even though he was very distant with me, I would just feel good that he was home. This went on for several months. I went to see Dr. Borror again. I told him about my daughter also moving out, and he advised me not to cut my daughter off but to walk in love. He reminded me that love can heal. That was a big order, but I somehow knew I would have to change my ways and listen to his advice. He shared these verses with me:

Hatred stirs up strife, but love covers all transgressions.
(Proverbs 10:12)

When there are many words, transgression is unavoidable, but
he who restrains his lips is wise. (Proverbs 10:19)

So, to obey God's Word, there needs to be dying to the flesh. On my way home, I prayed, "Lord, I want Your will for my life. I choose to obey, with Your help." And I cried.

When I got home, I made a big dinner. I don't even remember what I cooked but I do remember that it was more than enough for two people. I thought to myself, Why did I cook all this food for just Howard and me? I was then led to call my daughter. I called her at work (because I had her phone number there). When she answered, she was surprised to hear from me; I could tell it in her voice. I told her that I loved her and that I hoped she was okay. She said she was glad I called. I then asked her if she would like to come out and have dinner with us. She said yes, but then she hesitated and asked, "Can I bring Ron with me?" My heart sank as I had never met him, but it was as though the Holy Spirit took over, and I said, "Why sure." She sounded really happy about that. When I hung up, I cried out, "Oh Lord, help me be what You want me to be." It's really amazing how, when you ask the Lord for help, He provides the very thing you need.

Debbie and Ron came on a Tuesday evening before Howard came home. When they came to the door, I had the peace of God working in me. I opened the door and Debbie was standing there, but Ron kind of peeked around the corner of the house. I said, "Hi, Ron, I'm glad to meet you," which kind of shocked him. While we talked, the love of the Holy Spirit was evident in our conversation. Howard came home and was so kind to Ron and so glad to see Debbie. We ate dinner and then played a few games together and had a good time. And in those moments, God's peace just covered me. When they left, I knew I would be faced with Howard leaving again on Wednesday and my flesh would be in pain. But I was glad it opened the door of love to my daughter, even though she knew I did not approve of this relationship. It also sent an example of God's love to Ron, which caused him to see a reflection of a different kind of love in me. We had a long road ahead but God was at work.

Dr. Borror recommended that I see a female psychologist. The next day, I called the psychologist and made an appointment with her for that same afternoon. When I arrived, I could not hold back the tears. I was so broken, but God's love gets involved in a broken life. She just listened to my pain. She told me I would need to tell my husband to leave. She said, "Lorraine, you just can't live like this any longer." I cried and said, "No! No! I don't want to tell him to leave." But she quoted scripture: "I can do all things through Christ who strengthens me." I refused to say it, but she kept prodding me and said, "Lorraine, you can't live like this. God will help you." She again said, "Repeat this." So, through my tears, I repeated it. God was bottling up those tears, as He says in His Word, but I didn't know that at that time.

Well, it was God's Word, but little did I know that God was in control even at that time. Maybe it was the wrong counsel, but somehow I felt that God was still in control as He knew my heart. When I got home, I made dinner. It was a Wednesday evening, and after dinner Howard went to his recliner chair. I went to him and got down on my knees in front of him and I told him, "Howard, I just can't handle this anymore. You need to leave." He kind of jerked back in his chair and said nothing. I think it kind of shocked him, but then he got up and took most of his clothes out of the closet and put them in his car. He laid down for a few hours before he had to leave for work. I was in a daze and could not even lie down. I took valium to ease my pain. Howard couldn't really sleep either and finally got up and got ready for work. I wanted to stop him but he pulled away and said, "I have been thinking about this anyway."

After he left, I fell on the bed and sobbed, "God, this just isn't fair." I thrashed around until I was totally exhausted. Then I heard that still, small voice of the Holy Spirit. It sounded so kind, compassionate, and understanding, like He knew my pain. He said, "Lorraine, are you ready to listen to Me?" I said, "Oh Lord, yes, yes, yes!" I had my face down on the bed but I felt as if Jesus was kneeling by my bed at my head, as if He was kneeling down looking at me. I felt a surge of love surround me and compassion consume me. I wanted to raise my head to see His eyes looking at me, but I was afraid that if I didn't see Him I would think it was just my imagination. Then in an instant I just knew He was there, even if I did not see Him. I raised my head, my eyes all red and swollen. I was just so relaxed, I felt so much love, that I forgot my pain and fell into a deep sleep. But of course when I woke up, reality hit me again. Somehow, I knew God would be with me. As I opened my Bible, I came upon where Hannah made the vow:

> *She made a vow and said, "O LORD of hosts, if You will indeed look on the affliction of Your maidservant and remember me, and not forget Your maidservant, but will give Your maidservant a son, then I will give him to the LORD all the days of his life, and a razor shall never come on his head."* (1 Samuel 1:11)

But where she prayed for a son, I prayed for Howard: "Oh Lord of heaven, if You will look down upon my sorrow and answer my prayer, heal my marriage and bring my husband home, then I will release Howard into Your hands. He'll be Yours, because I can't change him."

4

Secluded

God's Molding

For several weeks, I did not leave the house. I began to read God's Word because I needed God's help. I opened the Bible and started to read. This is what God showed me:

> *This I recall to my mind, Therefore I have hope. The LORD'S loving kindnesses indeed never cease, for His compassions never fail. They are new every morning; great is Your faithfulness. "The LORD is my portion," says my soul, "Therefore I have hope in Him." The LORD is good to those who wait for Him, to the person who seeks Him. It is good that he waits silently for the salvation of the LORD.* (Lamentations 3:21-26)

> *The name of the LORD is a strong tower; the righteous runs into it and is safe.* (Proverbs 18:10)

Obey God even if you're not quite sure how it will turn out. Obedience is better than your sacrifice. The three young Hebrew men facing the fiery furnace said,

> *If we are thrown into the blazing furnace, the God we serve is able to deliver us from it, and he will deliver us from Your Majesty's hand. But even if he does not, we want you to know, Your Majesty, that we will not serve your gods or worship the image of gold you have set up.* (Daniel 3:17-18)

God was asking me through this situation if I was ready to take that stand for my marriage, believing all so that He can restore me, and not bow to the world's standards. I saw the title for one of the sections about forgiveness and faith and that caught my spirit. I really could not relate to the Bible for everyday life, even after all the Bible studies I had attended, but that was going to change.

I was reading in Luke 8:45-50 about the healing of the woman with the issue of blood and the raising of Jairus's daughter. God spoke to me in His Word when Jairus came down and fell at Jesus' feet and begged Him to come home with him as his only child was dying. Jesus set off with him, pushing through the crowd, but when He was apprehended by the woman with the issue of blood, He stopped to minister to her. While ministering to her, a messenger arrived from Jairus's home with the news that his little girl had died. The Bible reads, "There's no use troubling the Teacher now," but Jesus heard what was said and turned to the father and said, "Don't be afraid. Believe in Me." That's when the Holy Spirit spoke to me: "Consider this man. He was as human as you. Don't you think he became very nervous and afraid at this delay and would want to hurry Jesus along?" But it doesn't give us these details about his feelings or emotions or reactions in the Bible. Then I heard these words: "You have heard some devastating news. Don't be afraid. Believe in Me." Once again, I felt God's love all over me, but I didn't know what was ahead of me. I didn't know what God had planned for me—that He would teach me all I needed to know about faith in Him. God's Word was beginning to speak to me. I heard, "Keep planting your seed of love. All things are possible to him who believes."

Later, my friend Vickie called and wanted to see me, and she invited me to her prayer group. I declined to attend the prayer meeting at first because I just didn't want to mingle with people. She had served with me in Christian Women's Club as my assistant in the prayer ministry. My last year on the board, I was in charge of the witnessing booklets for the ministry; but during the last part of the year was when my trial really began. Vickie brought a little gift and asked me to come to her prayer group. The gift was a little flat iron booklet with a handle that lifted up; inside she had written a little note: "God is ironing all the wrinkles out of your life." I consented to attend her prayer group. They were familiar with the yellow booklet that contained testimonies of born-again marriages. Another friend, Louise, who I knew well and who attended the prayer group, wanted to give me the book right away but Vickie advised her to pray about it first.

Louise prayed and felt that God was leading her to bring me the booklet. She called one day and asked if she could come over and bring me something, as she was standing also for her second marriage. That was the beginning of the Lord sending me a great mentor. After reading the booklet, I began to have hope. Howard would drop by periodically, but he was always anxious to leave. He was spending most of his time in Arizona but had an apartment in Vernon, California, close to his work. Louise would come over and we would read and study that booklet together. We learned how to bind the enemy, which before I had not known anything about. Together we would attend meetings where healings took place and the baptism of the Holy Spirit was preached. I had a hard time with that because of where I had come from. I would call Louise when I would hear some bad news about Howard. I would tell her all the bad things and she would say, "Stop, Lorraine. We can't afford to get into a pity party. We need to pray for Howard. God knows what's going on in his life and you can't let the enemy take hold of your mind." Then she would pray and I would feel a release after her prayer.

As time went on, sometimes I would hear bad news and be upset and I'd call her to relate information and she'd stop me immediately. So I would hang up on her. I did this a couple of times. I would start to complain, but once she called back to apologize: "I'm sorry, Lorraine. Maybe I came down a little hard on you, but we need to pray and not confess these things as we can't afford a pity party." Then I remembered something that Dr. Borror would say: "Christians are not allowed the luxury of self-pity." I felt like I was a victim but I knew Louise always acted in love. We would get together often as she had become a woman of faith; she and Vickie both were my mentors. But I struggled with my flesh. Remember, in the stand we have three enemies: the world, the flesh, and the devil. I learned that if you yield to the flesh, the devil will move in—and boy, does he!

So shall they fear the name of the LORD from the west, and his glory from the rising of the sun. When the enemy shall come in like a flood, the Spirit of the LORD shall lift up a standard against him. (Isaiah 59:19)

I heard that Howard was taking the woman on a vacation, which really hurt. I decided that I would go out myself and have a great time. My thought was that if he was having a good time, then so would I. About this time, Louise called me to go out to dinner with her, as we had done often. While we were out, I told her of my decision: "I'm going to go buy some new clothes and I'm going out and I'm going to have a good time, like he is." She just listened to me and we spoke a bit, but then she interrupted me and said, "Lorraine, you can choose what you want to do, but I'm telling you that you will not find peace or happiness doing that. Believe me, I have been there. That's not the answer. I wouldn't do that if I was you, but God will let you choose.

But I'm going to pray for you." I was so angry. I thought, I'm going to do what I want to do. I'm tired of trying to be good. The next day I went to Zody's, a clothing store that was quite popular in California. I picked out a nice dress, shoes to match, some jewelry, and so forth. I was headed for the checkout stand when I heard the still, small voice: "You better put all those things back." I just kind of froze there and stood in a daze. Then I turned around and put one thing back after another. I walked out of the store, got in my car, dropped my head on the steering wheel, and cried. Don't underestimate prayer! I knew Louise was praying for me. God saved me from a very bad decision.

About this time, a friend invited me to attend Calvary Chapel in Downey with her. I declined at first, but I just couldn't attend the Baptist church where we had been going. It was just too painful to face my friends there. So I finally agreed to go with her. At that time, they were meeting in a large theater in Pico Rivera that wasn't too far from where I lived. I loved their music and the messages. My friend would pick me up and we would go together.

Eventually the church outgrew that theater, but the White Front store in Downey was up for sale. Calvary Chapel put in a bid and got the building, which was a miracle for Calvary Chapel. They converted one end of the large building into the sanctuary. I felt the Spirit so strong in that church. They also opened a chapel store and I loved to browse in there. They had a department where they would lend out Jeff's taped messages for a week, which I would return the next Sunday. I did not own a cassette player at that time, so I decided to go out to look for one.

I ended up finding one for around $90, so I put it on a credit card and could hardly wait to get home and check out Jeff's messages. But when I got home, the Lord reminded me, "That was wrong. If you are going to spend

that much money, you need to approach your husband first."
That really set me back as I thought that he would never
go for spending that kind of money. He wasn't giving me
any money anyway and I was feeling pretty bad. I just sat
there. I just couldn't use it. I thought that was very unfair
and I wasn't sure which way to go. Then I heard, "Return
it and do the right thing." That sent chills through me.
How could I do that? Finally, because I felt so miserable
about it, I decided that I had better go ahead and obey the
prompting. When I got to the store, there was a long line
of people returning things. I prayed, "Lord, please don't
let her ask me why I'm returning this." I hoped no one
would stand behind me, which no one did. But there were
two lines of people and one across from me, so if she asked
me, they would hear our conversation. Then I heard, "Just
tell the truth." Oh boy, God was doing His work in my life.

So, when I walked up to the girl, I handed her the
cassette player and the receipt and told her I was returning
it. You guessed it, she asked, "What's the problem?" I
froze for a second and then said, "You see, I did not ask my
husband if I could get this. As it cost more than $50, I should
ask him first." She went off on a tirade and embarrassed
me: "I don't see why you need to ask him. Boy, if I want
something I'm not going to ask my husband first. If I can
do that or get that, no way." But I calmly replied, "If you
want a good marriage, you need to let your husband be the
head of the house. That's what I am learning now about
how to have a successful marriage." She didn't accept that
very well but she removed it from my credit card. I went
home feeling relieved but kind of sad. I had really wanted
to listen to those tapes.

Howard dropped by as he occasionally did. He wanted
to look at something in the TV department at Target. He
asked me if I would like to go along. I was always happy
to be with him. While he was looking at the things he was

interested in (I don't remember what that was), my eyes fell on the cassette players. I was looking at them when he came over to me. I remarked how nice they were and wondered if he would let me get one. "Well, let's look at them," he said. They had one on a stand that was a double-cassette player, radio and record player all in one. He asked, "Do you like this one?" I couldn't believe my ears! I said, "Yes, that is a really nice one." He told the clerk, "We want this unit." I was just overcome with emotion. It was nicer than the one that I had picked. God is a good Father, even though sometimes His instructions hurt at the moment! Well, I began checking out Jeff's taped messages, bringing them home and listening to them over and over all week. I copied them with my double-tape deck. Wow, did I get filled with God's Word! But little did I know the road that was ahead for me.

5

Intervention

God's Love

A fter receiving the yellow booklet and getting acquainted with a born-again marriage ministry that was located in Council Bluffs, Iowa, I began to contact them for encouragement and prayer. I prayed that they would come to California and start group meetings out here, and it came to pass. I then became involved in the intercessory prayer ministry with them. I'd pray for marriages all across the country, as they would send me a list of couples that needed prayer. All the while, I was still at home trying to get my emotions, fears, and hurts together.

I had some physical problems at that time also. I had injured my back a few years earlier before our trial began and had been doctoring it, but then it got worse. I could hardly stand, sit, or lie down, as I was in so much pain. The doctor told me that I had ruptured a disc and that I most likely would need surgery on my back. In addition to the physical pain in my back, I was suffering the pain of my troubled marriage.

One day Louise came over and asked me to go with her to visit our friend Vickie, just to get me out of the house for a while. I really did not want to go because of the pain, but she persisted and said, "Just for a little while." So I consented. I was really miserable because I couldn't find relief sitting, standing, or even lying on the floor; I tried everything. Finally, Louise decided we better leave and go home, but they said, "Let's pray first before you go." We got into a circle and I sat on a chair in front of Vickie and Louise, and they began to pray for me. Then Vickie stopped and said the Lord told her to put my feet on her lap. She noticed that one of my legs was a bit shorter than the other, not sure if that was due to my injury. They then began praying in their heavenly language. As they laid their hands on my legs, I was very skeptical about this but I didn't say anything to them. All of a sudden, it felt like someone was pulling on my leg and my hip hurt so bad. I wanted to let go of their hands and grab my hip, but I didn't. I just had to grit my teeth and hold on. Then I heard my shoes squeak as my feet were close together. I thought this was strange, but then the pain left. I said nothing and they kept on praying. Once again, the same thing happened. I peeked to see if they were pulling on my leg, but their hands were just lying on my leg. I had no idea what was happening. Then the sound of my shoes squeaked again and I started to laugh. I didn't know why, but I couldn't stop laughing. They kept on praying until they started to laugh too. Then I just blurted out, "God has healed me!" I got up from the chair and walked around. I sat down and I got up—no more pain! I was just praising the Lord. We all were!

From that time on, I had no more pain. It was the miracle of healing. God was merciful to me as I obeyed their leading, even with my skeptical attitude, disapproval of their praying in tongues, and so forth. God overlooked my fear and disbelief and touched my body.

I started attending meetings with Born Again Marriages, which was started in Lake Forrest, California. Many people attended those meetings and we were all encouraged by the Word of God. This was when I met Marilyn Conrad, as she too was involved with Born Again

Marriages. She came out to visit the group I was attending. We undergirded one another, we studied the Word, but we did not discuss our mates or our problems, but we did pray for them and for ourselves. I would always come home uplifted with hope and peace. I was studying and reading the Word and came across verses that really confused me.

We proclaim Him, admonishing every man and teaching every man with all wisdom, so that we may present every man complete in Christ. (Colossians 1:28)

This verse bothered me. I thought, I want to be complete (perfect) but how can I be? So, I called the leader of the ministry, Kent, to ask him if he could explain that scripture to me, as it concerned me. He explained it to me, and then said he would look into it more and explain it to me in more detail on a cassette and mail it to me.

He asked me if I had received the baptism of the Holy Spirit. I was very skeptical about it and said no. Then he asked if I would you like to receive the baptism of the Holy Spirit now. I was confused and didn't want to because I didn't believe in it. So I hesitated for a little bit because I wasn't sure, but finally I said, "Okay." Kent said he was going to pray and said I should do the same. He started praying but I just sat there because I couldn't. But then I felt the power of the Holy Spirit on me and I started to pray. Finally, when I hung up, I was full of joy, the joy of the Lord. I was just elated. I don't know how to explain it. I just felt the power of God all over me, as though I was right in the presence of God. From that point on, God took over my life. That was when I really learned the power of the Holy Spirit in my life. The Bible teaches about the baptism of the Holy Spirit, like when they were in the upper room and the Holy Spirit came on everybody. But I needed that in my life. God knew that, even in my moment of skepticism, confusion and fear. Isn't God good with His children? I guess I was like doubting Thomas, who wouldn't believe until he could touch the holes in Christ's hands.

About this time, I needed to find a job because Howard was not supporting me in any way. I was frightened and didn't know what to look for, with no experience outside the home. I got a job with a greeting-card company in the greeting and wrapping-paper department, and all that went with that department; I provided service to five drugstores for their card department. I worked for several months with this but wasn't generating enough income, as I was only working about 20 hours a week. So I decided to go back to work at the local school cafeteria, where I had worked for seven years while the children were in school. Howard had approved of my leaving that job, as he had wanted me to stay home and look after the home and children. That was the way we grew up in our hometown. But the Lord blessed me with the card position, as my trainer and boss really liked me.

One day she said, "Lorraine, I have a lot of clothes I do not wear anymore and I believe they would fit you. Can I bring them to you the next time I come to the store?" She had a big box full of clothes. I was just in awe when I went through the beautiful clothes: casual pants, nice pants, pant sets, blouses, and so forth. Every one of them fit me. I felt overjoyed as I had never had clothes quite like she had given me.

I was hoping that when Howard would drop by he'd be amazed at how nice I looked. He was, but he still didn't show any emotion for me and was always so quick to leave. I then moved on and put my application in for the cafeteria work and was hired immediately due to my experience. I was at least working five days a week. I was having some very painful days though, because of Howard's attitude and actions toward me. After a year in the cafeteria, a friend called me who was working as a crossing guard and told me that they were hiring crossing guards in Long Beach.

She suggested that I should go and put my application in, and I did. I resigned the cafeteria job and was hired by the Long Beach Police Department. The City of Long Beach furnished all of our uniforms, shirt, pants, jacket, and a yellow jacket, which was really good. I was in training and filled in wherever they needed me. Toward the end of the second year of training, I was put on a corner no other crossing guard wanted: the corner of Market and Locust. Many children crossed on this corner, and I was very nervous as I had no idea where all these children came from. I wasn't sure which side of the street I would belong, but the Lord calmed my fears and gave me His promises that He would be with me. After a few days, I got the hang of it and began to realize where I needed to sit: right across from the liquor store. I finished out that year at five and a half hours a day. When it was time to go back in the fall, I begged God to give me a better corner. When we had our first meeting of all crossing guards at the Police Department in Long Beach, they put up the corners that were up for bid. There were a couple I really wanted to get on, but because I was just a new guard, there were many people with seniority. You guessed it, I wound up back on the same corner. I was not happy about that but I made up my mind to do the best I could, do my job well, and hope that the next year would be different. Well, before the year was up, they increased my hours to six hours and I was happy about that, but I was still hopeful to get another corner with more hours. God had other plans for me.

In the morning, as I would get ready for work, the 700 Club would come on at 6 a.m. and I would have to leave at 6:30 a.m. for work. I would turn on the TV after I was ready for work and would watch the show for that half hour. They talked about marriage and how God could restore marriages in trouble, so I started listening to this every day. One particular day there was a pledge taking place. In my spirit, I knew God was asking me to take a step of faith and pledge $100 for my restored marriage. My thought was, One hundred dollars? Where will I get $100? So I just shut the TV off and went to work. I didn't think about it anymore. The next morning, I turned the TV on once again and the pledge was still taking place. People were sharing how God was answering their prayers. Once again, I heard God ask me to pledge $100 but I just shut the TV off again and went to work. But I couldn't get away from the thought of what God was asking me to do in faith. The next morning, I decided not to turn on the TV because I did not want to hear God ask me again to pledge $100; but curiosity got the best of me and I turned on the TV again. The thought came back into my mind and I felt a little angry because I did not know where I would get $100. I shut the TV off again!

The next day was the final day of the telethon, and I hesitated to turn on the TV. But I did. God was leading me to obey, and my thought was that I had better obey God. Although I didn't know where the money would come from, I decided to step out in faith. I called and made my pledge for a healed marriage. I received prayer for God to answer my request. One week went by, two weeks went by, three weeks went by, four weeks went by and I began to panic because I didn't know where I would get the money. Then I questioned God, for surely they would think I lied about pledging the money. I tried to figure out how to come up with $100—maybe a garage sale? What could I sell to raise $100? I heard God say, "Trust Me." But that really frustrated me, because I was trying to figure out where the money would come from. I called my friend and asked her for advice on what I should do. I said, "I don't want to tell you what I did; I just don't know what to do." Her reply was, "What did God tell you to do?" I hesitated for a minute since that bothered me. I then told her that God had asked me to trust Him. Once again she said, "Isn't that what you should do then?" and we ended our conversation with prayer. At that point, I said, "Okay, God, I will trust You."

Only a few days later, I received a call from Howard. He asked how I was doing, and we talked briefly, and then he said he was sending me $200. I would have to drive to Whittier to pick up the money, but $100 was for me to pay bills and the other $100 was for whatever I wanted. When I hung up, I knew: there was my $100. I struggled for a long time, not knowing how God would provide; little did I know that God would use my own husband to provide the money for a pledge I had made to have our marriage restored. Now, don't tell me that God doesn't work in strange ways. Who would have thought that God would use my husband to provide the money? That was the last thing on my mind. God told me to pledge the money. I didn't think of doing that, but God would be the one to provide the money. That was such a lesson on obedience to God!

I had been attending meetings with Born Again Marriage ministry. I wanted to give more into the ministry but I didn't have the finances to do it. Then I heard in my spirit, "You have something in your cupboard that's just collecting dust and tarnish." I was set back by that thought. *I thought, Now why would I even think that? Furthermore, that doesn't make sense. What would they do with a sterling silver set like that?* I tried to get that out of my mind. Every time I would think, *I'd sure like to give them more money, but I don't have it to give,* the thought would pop into my mind again. Our children had given this to us on our 25th anniversary! I couldn't figure out how they could possibly use this and I tried to push it out of my mind once more, but the Lord kept bringing it back. I struggled hard with that. On my way to church on a Sunday morning, I prayed, "Lord, whatever You want me to hear this morning, I will listen." In the pastor's message, he talked about obeying God, and he said, "I think there is someone here who God is speaking to but you're trying to avoid it." I felt as though that message was aimed right at me.

On my way home, I cried and said, "Okay, Lord, I will obey You even though this really bothers me." When I got home, I pulled the set from the cupboard and said, "Okay, God, I sure don't understand this but I will obey You." I really didn't want to part with that set as the children had given it to us, but I chose to obey the voice of the Lord. On Monday morning, I called Janeen to ask her if she could tell me how to get in touch with the head of the ministry, but when I dialed her number the head of the ministry himself answered. When I told him what the Lord wanted me to do, he was surprised to hear that but said that I should bring it down to the meeting. They were going to have Wednesday night service at a church in Costa Mesa. By this time, I did have peace of mind about this, so I took it down.

A young man who was standing for his marriage came to my car and carried it in. I was able to meet the leaders after the meeting. They ministered to others and wanted to pray with me. They said they would do with the sterling silver set what God wanted them to do with it. When I started home after the service, I was really attacked by the enemy, for he said, "Your children are going to be very angry with you, as this surely doesn't have anything to do with your marriage." I got a knot in my stomach and thought, Oh my goodness, what have I done? I then remembered a message that I had heard about the enemy coming in to try to get you off course. I realized I needed to take authority and I told Satan in Jesus' name, "Get out of my life. I am obeying God. You're not going to put fear in me," and I felt freedom instantly.

That Friday evening Born Again Marriages was having another meeting in Century City. A friend who was standing for her marriage called me and wanted to know if I was going to go. I told her no because I had been to the meeting in Costa Mesa. She asked if I would please go and drive and we would share the gas. I agreed. When we got to the meeting, there was a large crowd. A lady came up to me and said, "Lorraine, we want you in the front row." I wondered why as I was sitting with some friends, and the front row had already filled up. Well, they came and got me and put me in the second row. At the end of the meeting, the leader said, "Lorraine, we want you to come up here." I thought, Oh my goodness, why do they want me up there? She said, "Come on, Lorraine." I went up and she told me to close my eyes and said, "You are an intercessor and intercessors don't peek. Don't open your eyes until we tell you to." I felt a bit awkward but I waited. And then she said, "Open your eyes." When I opened my eyes, here came that same young man, walking down the aisle carrying my sterling silver coffee and tea set. They said to me, "God told us to give it back to you." At this point tears filled my eyes. I thought about God testing my obedience by having me release something that I greatly treasured. He was testing to see if I was willing to obey.

Then one of the leaders said, "Before you leave here tonight, you're going to receive a car." I needed a car very much. I thought, *Who in the world would give me a car here?* Gavin and Patty McLeod were sitting in the front row. Patty stood up and asked if she could come up and say something, and they invited her to come up. She had been standing and praying for Gavin to come home and for God to restore their marriage. She pointed to Gavin and told everyone, "My husband is here with me tonight. He has returned home." She said that they had two cars and didn't really need two cars. They had been praying about

giving it to someone in the ministry, and when the leader had spoken of me receiving a car, Gavin had leaned over to Patty and had said, "That is where the Cadillac goes." She said, "Lorraine, you got your car." I was dumbfounded. I just didn't know what to say. A date was set for me to pick it up. I asked a friend to go with me as I wasn't sure I'd be able to operate a car like that. I had to go to work and I thought, *Lord, what am I going to say to people? I'm a crossing guard and here I drive up in a Cadillac. What do I say?* I heard, "Tell the truth." I thought, *Oh my goodness, I can't tell them that I got a car from You, that You allowed me to receive this car.* God reminded me to tell the truth. So when I got to work and people asked, "Oh, my goodness, what did you get?" I just swallowed and said, "The Lord gave it to me through someone else." That seemed to satisfy them.

A few days later Howard called. I didn't want to tell him that I had been given a Cadillac. But I knew I couldn't keep it in, so I said to him, "I got something." He asked, "What?" When I said, "I got a Cadillac," there was silence on the other end of the phone. Finally, he said, "Run that by me again?" I said, "I got a Cadillac." Then he told me he would be down to see me, and sure enough, he came to see the Cadillac.

That spring we had our high school reunion in South Dakota, and he decided that he and I were going to drive the Cadillac back to our high school reunion. We had a chance to see all our friends, and we were also able to spend time with our families. It brought back so many memories about the years we had spent together. We ended up having a very good time.

6

Experiencing Love

God's Mercy

The crossing guard job was where God built my character and taught me how to walk in love, especially with the unlovely. I had a little Jesus promise book that I carried with me along with a small book called Favor the Road to Success by Bob Buess. When I would run into situations that I would not know how to handle, I would go to these little books and find the scripture that would give me a word to apply to the situation and the correction I would need.

Sometimes I would have difficulty with the children. One particular incident was with a little boy who would not cross the street in the crosswalk with me. I would get so

upset with him that I would scold him. The other kids would ask me, "How come he can cross on the other side of the street and we can't?" Sometimes he just ran across the street before I even crossed with the other children! I would panic because he wouldn't look for cars; he would just look at me and laugh. I would just get serious with him; I would tell the other kids that was disobedience and it would get him in trouble. They would agree, which eased my mind that perhaps no one would follow his mindset.

I dreaded going to work. I just didn't know how to handle that boy. I prayed at night and in the morning, "God, please help me with this child before he has an accident. I would not be able to handle that." Finally, after about a week of this, the Lord spoke to me and said:

Do not be overcome by evil, but overcome evil with good. (Romans 12:21)

I asked, "Lord, how do I do that?" and God responded with "Try walking in love." But I didn't know how to do that. God reminded me that when I get angry and upset, I'm not showing love. I prayed, asking God to please help me; I felt so frustrated and inadequate, but God knew that. I surrendered to the Holy Spirit and walked in love. The little boy obeyed and followed instructions.

Let no one say when he is tempted, "I am being tempted by God"; for God cannot be tempted by evil, and He Himself does not tempt anyone. (James 1:13)

That meant to take authority over the enemy, who is using that child to cause me problems.

Now as to the love of the brethren, you have no need for anyone to write to you, for you yourselves are taught by God to love one another. (1 Thessalonians 4:9)

I prayed again to God that morning. The little boy came and stopped on the opposite side of the street as usual.

I told him good morning and smiled at him. He waited until I crossed the other children and then crossed on the opposite side again. As always, I told the other children to have a good day. Then I called out to the little boy, "Have a good day, son." I had taken authority over Satan's control of that little boy.

Every day I prayed and I responded in that way. I don't now recall how many days, but it was enough for God to help me control my impatience and emotions toward that little boy, to stay in His love. Finally, one morning he came across the street and walked with me and the other children across the street. God was at work in my life. I would give the children some candy and stickers with "Jesus loves you" or "Jesus is Lord" on them. But the enemy first put fear in me about losing my job when I first started to do this.

In fact, the first time I bought the candy, little Hershey bars individually wrapped, and the stickers, fear gripped me. On my break time, I took them home and put them in the refrigerator so they wouldn't melt and then went back to work. I was walking up and down on the sidewalk praying when the Holy Spirit prompted me: was I concerned about what man would think or was I trusting God? Well, He convicted me again. I prayed, "Oh God, forgive me for yielding to fear." After crossing all the children for school, I had a 15-minute break. I got in my car, went home, and got the candy and stickers. I went back to my corner, ready for the rest of the children to give them their stickers and candy.

That started a ministry: all holidays, Valentine's Day, Easter, spring break, the last day of school, the first day of school, Halloween, Thanksgiving, and Christmas. The children all just loved it. I crossed between 350 and 400 children a day. The next year again I pleaded with

God, "Please let me get a different corner." I didn't want to go back to that corner. When we had our meeting for all guards in the fall for the new year, they had a list of corners up for bid. I put my bid in on a corner that I'd like to work at, but again some other guard with more seniority would get it, and back I'd go to that corner. I was so disappointed and dreaded going back because it was a very dangerous corner! There were no signal lights to help, and on foggy days it was very scary and I had to be very cautious.

I accepted my position, even though I was not doing it in the right attitude, but I started off with my same routine. I saw some pretty bad things take place around that liquor store, but I would claim God's promise to protect me. I would make this confession every morning when I arrived at my corner:

This is the day which the LORD has made; Let us rejoice and be glad in it. (Psalm 118:24)

My soul exalts the Lord, and my spirit has rejoiced in God my Savior. (Luke 1:46-47) *My son, do not reject the discipline of the LORD Or loathe His reproof, for whom the LORD loves He reproves, even as a father corrects the son in whom he delights.* (Proverbs 3:11-12)

Thank You, Lord! The Holy Spirit dwells in me. He gives me wisdom and His divine love and forgiveness. Peace and joy operate in me. I am the righteousness of God because of Jesus; therefore, I can say that God's eyes are over me and His ears are open to my prayers just as 1 Peter 3:12 reminds me. I am also heir of God, joint heir of Jesus Christ; I have Christ's love, faith, forgiveness, understanding, discernment, patience, tenderness, and compassion operating in me. In 2 Corinthians 9:8, God's promise is that His grace enables me for it and abounds to me in every good work. I surrender my thoughts, attitudes, imagination to Him. I dedicate my heart and my tongue to Him. I have health and wealth, spiritually, physically and materially, because I have God's Word.

Give and it shall return; love and it shall return. I'm entitled to God's grace, mercy, and favor. Psalm 5:12 reminds me of His goodness and that His mercy shall follow me. I have favor with God and man according to Proverbs 12:2 and Proverbs 8:35. I receive and believe that all my needs are met. Jesus, You say no evil will befall me, neither any plague come near my dwelling, and I agree with His Word. Where there is unforgiveness, now there is love. Where there is bitterness, now there is reconciliation. Where there is poverty in our relationship, now there is abundance. Where there is unforgiveness, now there is forgiveness. For nothing shall be impossible with God. For I dwell under the shadow of the Almighty, as Psalm 91 reminds me. His wings shield me and shelter me, and His faithful promises are my armor.

Now it's year number three, and once again I asked the Lord to let me get on another corner. But if I wanted the same hours, I would have to be on the same corner. When it was time for the meeting at the police station, the corners were once again up for bid—not very many though, so I was concerned that I would be disappointed again. Sure enough, I had to return to the same corner. I cried out to God on my way home from the meeting, "Oh God, I just don't want to go back there again!" The next morning, as I was getting ready for work, I dropped to my knees and said, "Okay, Lord, if this is your assignment for me, I will accept it. I won't complain anymore. I will do my job well with Your help for as long as You want me there." Peace filled my being and I felt a release from my struggle with this corner; from there I looked forward to what God had in store for me.

When I got to work, children started coming, and every one who came hugged me and told me how glad they were that I was back as their crossing guard. I was just blown away by their reactions. I finally learned their names and started to call them by name. Every morning the parents were amazed at how I could remember all their names, even the toddlers the mothers had in their strollers to cross with me. God was my source in everything, in my memory as well. A couple of weeks into the school year, my supervisor came out and told me they were going to increase my hours to six and a half because I had so many children. God was blessing me. One day the principal of the school came to me and mentioned that, although she didn't know what I was doing, the children really liked me and talked about me a lot. I just told her that it was God who put me on that corner, that I had finally accepted it, and that He was my helper.

She just smiled. I began to share the Lord with parents and children. I was even asked to pray. There were a couple of incidents but one in particular happened when the children were heading home from school one day. A couple of junior high girls got into a bad fight, right by the liquor store. They pulled each other's hair and scratched each other's face. One girl grabbed the other by the hair and slammed her head into the wall of the liquor store. A couple of boys pulled up in their car, jumped on their trunk, and egged the girls on. One little girl who I witnessed to about the Lord came over to my car and asked me to do something. I was sitting in my car at the time and was scared to get out of my car as I didn't have any children to cross at that time. I was shaking but I felt the Lord prodding me to go to them. The minute I stepped out of my car, the fear left me. I walked across the street and put my arm around one of the girls and told her that God loved her and so did I. She pulled away and looked at me in astonishment and then walked away. The two boys jumped off the car and drove off. I went to the other girl, whose face was bleeding from scratches and her hair was a mess—the one who had her head knocked into the wall. I put my arm around her and told her that God loved her and so did I. "You don't need to fight, whatever this is about." She dropped her head on my shoulder and started to cry. I hugged her and held her for a while. She then headed home and seemed to be okay.

It was about time then for me to go on my break, and as I started, the Lord asked me to give her one of those little booklets. "Oh Lord, I didn't think of that! Well, I don't know how to find her now." But I felt led to try. I went around the block and started down the street but couldn't see her. Then suddenly she came out into my path. I stopped and called, and she came over to the car. I gave her the little witnessing booklets I carried with me. She thanked me and once again I told her I loved her and that God would be with her. She reached in the car and gave me a hug. Every day she would ask her little sister to tell me hello. Today, that girl works at a restaurant near me! Many years later, I was in there with a friend for lunch and she waited on us. I did not recognize her; she is now married with two children of her own. When she came to our table, she looked at me and told me I looked familiar: "I know you from someplace; you a schoolteacher?" I said, "No, but I was a crossing guard on Market and Locust." She just grabbed me and hugged me and said, "That's it! Yes, yes, you were my crossing guard!"

A friend I knew from Christian Women's Club was a freelance writer. She came to my corner and wanted to write an article about my crossing guard work. She wanted me to tell how God was using me on this corner. I wasn't too excited about saying anything and didn't even know what to tell her. She asked me a few questions and I told her a few things about what God was doing with me as I struggled with the pain of my marriage and having to work. She wrote an article and sent it to Moody Monthly magazine, and she took a picture of me crossing the children. Well, the article was accepted at Moody Monthly and she received $75 for the article. She came and gave me all the money to buy the things that I was giving out to the children, as she said she wanted to help support my ministry with these children.

My corner was not far from the fire department in that area. One morning as I was standing on my corner, the fire truck went by and pulled over to the curve. The driver jumped out and asked me if I was the crossing guard who was in the Moody Monthly article. I said yes. He said, "I want you to know that I am praying for you. God bless your work on this corner."

God was busy changing my life and helping me cope with the pain of my marriage. I would pray for my husband, family, relatives, and all marriages. On my two-hour break time in the morning, I would go to a nearby Kmart parking lot, park in a space where there were no other cars, get in the backseat of my car, and pray, pray, pray. Sometimes I would cry. One evening when I got home from work, which was about 6 p.m., I received a phone call from a family member. She told me about some of the things that Howard was doing. I know she did not mean to hurt me; she just thought that I should know what was going on. Howard's family thought I was foolish to be standing for my marriage. That night I called out to God and I cried and cried. I couldn't sleep. The next morning, I did not want to go to work because I was too upset. I was angry and hurt but I didn't feel I could call and ask for the day off. In tears I got ready, crying as I was driving to work. I glanced down and, between my seats, was a card I had received from Haven of Rest. The card reminded me to, in everything, give thanks, for this is the will of God in Christ Jesus for me. I was angry at those words and I wondered how I could give thanks for this as it just didn't make sense. I didn't want to even look at those words again, but the Holy Spirit caused me to glance down at them again, and of course I read them. And this thought came to me: Those are from God's Word, so maybe you had better obey them. I lifted one hand up, keeping the other on the steering wheel, and through my tears I said, "Okay, God, I thank You for what I heard. I thank You for what's going on. I thank You for my husband and for this job." All of a sudden, I was raptured into God's presence and I felt the joy of the Lord just consume me. By the time I reached my corner and parked, I had asked the Lord to allow my eyes to not look like I had been crying so that no one would know. I got out of my car and I just wanted to hug and love everyone who came to my corner. God was in the process of teaching me obedience to His Word and changing my attitude.

These are the words that God spoke to me when I got home from work. I was reading a little book called *God at Eventide* and I heard God speak to me in my desperate situation.

I control your thoughts. I inspire your impulses. I guide your footsteps. And I thanked God. I am trusting You, Lord. *I will strengthen your body, your mind, and your spirit. I am the link between you and those who are in the unseen. I am the love of your life, controller of your destiny, guardian, advocate, provider, and friend.*

That was an uplifting and encouraging message. When you seek Him, you will find Him, just as He says.

I heard that the Full Gospel Businessmen were having an event at the Anaheim Convention Center, and I wanted to attend but didn't want to go alone. I called my mentor, Louise, and I asked if she would go with me. Sadly, she was not able to go as she had other plans. As usual, her advice was to just go, that I wasn't alone as God is always with me. I really didn't know if I wanted to but I felt it in my heart to go, so I went. When I  walked in, I felt the presence of the Lord. The worship team was practicing and it just sent my heart soaring. I walked through the booths before the meeting and discovered a big truck in the area called the Spirit of the Road.

The ministry was Christian Truckers Association, founded by Jim and Alameda Keys. They would take their truck and minister to truckers throughout the country, providing  church services. I met with them and shared my dilemma. They prayed for me and for Howard. I got involved with this ministry and became a distributor for their Wheels Alive newspapers. I placed them in truck stops throughout Southern California. Truckers would grab those papers as fast as I would put them down. I also got involved with the board in California.

Lorraine Woodhouse — West Coast Distributor of Wheels Alive Magazine

One night I turned the TV on to Fred Price's ministry. That night he had Kenneth W. Hagan on. At the end of the message, he asked if anyone would like the anointing of God on their life. People responded. He said, "You out there, in TV land, raise your hands to the TV, and as I pray, God will anoint you." So I did. He began to pray and, all of a sudden, my hands got hot. I jerked them away because I didn't understand what was happening. As soon as I did, the heat went away. I asked the Lord what was happening; I didn't understand what this was or what it meant.

A few weeks later I was driving to Camarillo, California, to visit my daughter and her husband. I was passing a lot of trucks on the drive over. The Lord said, "I anointed your hands." He asked me to raise my hand toward the trucks and pray for their salvation. With one hand on the steering wheel and the other raised toward the truckers, I prayed. Sometimes they would wave at me. Sometimes I couldn't even take my hand down as there were so many trucks. From that time on, every time I was on the road, I prayed for the truckers.

Each year God was showing me how to walk with Him on the corner where He had placed me. I had a daily confession that I made each day because I never knew what I would be facing that day. I needed God's help, support, and wisdom each day. Jesus had sent the Holy Spirit to be in me and to be my helper. This was my confession: "Today will be a great day, for this is the day the Lord has made. I will rejoice and be glad in it. No matter what the day will bring."

For the Scripture says, "Whoever believes in him will not be disappointed." (Romans 10:11)

One thing I can say is that Jesus is my Savior, Lord of my life, and sovereign over all the affairs of my life. Therefore, I expect His help, guidance, instruction, and correction in my life.

My son, do not forget my teaching, but let your heart keep my commandments. (Proverbs 3:1)

Take hold of instruction; do not let go. Guard her, for she is your life. (Proverbs 4:13)

Behold, how happy is the man whom God reproves, So do not despise the discipline of the Almighty. For He inflicts pain, and gives relief; He wounds, and His hands also heal. From six troubles He will deliver you, even in seven evil will not touch you. (Job 5:17-19)

And God is able to make all grace abound to you, so that always having all sufficiency in everything, you may have an abundance for every good deed. (2 Corinthians 9:8)

One evening my niece called and told me that Howard was taking this woman and her family on vacation. When I hung up the phone, I was very angry, and I just wanted to beat my husband up. Occasionally he would stop by, and I thought, If he comes through that door, I'm going to let him have it! I was so angry and miserable. But the Lord stopped me and reminded me of this scripture:

Let all bitterness and wrath and anger and clamor and slander be put away from you, along with all malice. Be kind to one another, tender-hearted, forgiving each other, just as God in Christ also has forgiven you. (Ephesians 4:31-32)

I was set back by that, and when God reminded me of Proverbs 29:22, I knew that I was sinning as much as Howard was and that convicted me. I began to cry and asked the Lord to forgive me. I lifted my hands and held them up, telling God everything. I told Him everything that I had heard, everything that was said; and I told Him that I couldn't handle it anymore. I threw my hands up and said, "You take them, Lord!" And as God is my witness, it was like He poured a bucket of love over me. I would have hugged my husband if he had come through the door right then. What a transformation God did in my life at that time—and what a transformation He continued to do.

At the corner where I worked as a crossing guard, there was a little lady who lived across the street from where I parked. She lived in a little house behind a business in which she sold candy. There was a little fence on the side of the building with a small area of grass. Every morning when I pulled up to work, she would come out by the fence and wave at me. One day when I pulled up, she came out, and we said good morning to each other. When I got some of the children across the street, the Lord told to me give her $20. My thought was, Lord, all I have in my billfold is $20. What will I live on for the next few days? But I didn't hear anything. I crossed some more children and this thought just stayed with me. Finally, when I got all the children across, I went to the back to my car, got my billfold out, and took out the $20. I struggled with this, but I felt that God was leading me to do this. I went across the street, knocked on the little lady's door, and handed her the $20. I told her that the Lord wanted me to give this to her. She started to cry and she said, "I didn't know how I was going to buy groceries for myself this week." When I went back across the street, I started to cry, thinking how God knows everything about everybody and how He encourages us to step out and help. I was very touched that I obeyed God and that God supplied my needs.

A man was sitting behind the building when I pulled up the next day. He had a drinking problem and was lying on the ground against an empty building. I did not want to put up with his drinking in public while the kids were coming in; I was just frustrated with that. So, when the kids started coming to school, they looked at him and then looked at me, and I encouraged them not to pay any attention to him. When I was done crossing the children, I went back to my car and sat down for a few minutes. The Lord spoke to me and asked me to tell that man that God loved him and so did I. I didn't want to talk to that man. I thought he would probably throw the bottle at me.

The Lord just kept laying it on my heart and I kept feeling convicted. Finally, I went over to him, leaned down, and told him that God loved him and so did I. The man looked up at me with tears in his eyes and said, "I don't know why I do this. I have a wonderful wife and a wonderful family." He threw the bottle across the parking lot. I handed him a little witnessing card. The card read, "Angels are watching over you." He just started to cry. I asked him if I could pray for him and he said, "Please do." I didn't know what to pray, but the Holy Spirit took over and I prayed for him. He just hugged me afterward and asked if I had another one of those little cards as he wanted to give one to his wife. So I gave him another card and he left. I continued to pray for him after he left.

A few weeks later a lady came to my car and I recognized her: I crossed her three little girls. She told me that although she didn't know what I said to her husband, she wanted to thank me. Her husband had not had a drink since then and had been working every day. I told her I just prayed with him and shared the Lord. I encouraged her to give God the glory for touching her husband's life. She just wanted to thank me for taking the time to talk with him. I was so touched when she left that I broke out in tears at the thought that God knew this man. He was the father of these three little girls who I crossed and God was interested in someone talking with him. I was just touched by how God calls us to do things that we ordinarily would not do. I just saw how God was changing my life by walking in love, sharing His love with others, and how God intervened in their lives. I praised the Lord for what He was doing in my life.

Twenty years later, after I had retired, I was amazed at how God showed me that by being obedient to Him a life can be touched. God can help us through whatever our trouble is; alcohol can't. I had a phone call from a man named Juan, who asked if I was Lorraine Woodhouse. I answered with yes. He went on to say that I probably didn't remember him but that he had never forgotten me. He asked me if he could come over and see me, and if he could bring his wife; he wanted me to meet her. He didn't realize that I already had. I said yes, and they came over. We had a nice visit and they wanted to see me again in the near future. We go out to dinner once in a while.

At the corner where I worked, there was a young lady named Wanda who would come down to the liquor store. She would usually only buy a few groceries and then she would leave and go home. Wanda's husband worked at the convalescent home across the street, and some days before he had to go to work, she, her husband, and her two little girls would go to the park for a picnic. I would sit back and think to myself, What a lovely family; look at how happy they are. They had two beautiful little girls and seemed to be just a happy family.

One morning Wanda came to the liquor store to get something and the Lord asked me to give her one of the little witnessing booklets I carried around with me from Christian Women's Club. I questioned why I should give Wanda one of those booklets; she looked very happy. I brushed it off and didn't do it. Then a few days later she came down again and I heard the same thing, to give Wanda one of those little booklets. I thought, Okay, Lord, I don't understand this but I will do what You tell me. I walked across the street and handed Wanda the little booklet. I told her, "I don't know why, but the Lord just wants me to give this to you." She thanked me and said that she would read it.

Later that afternoon, Wanda came back down to my car and started to cry. She said, "Oh, Lorraine, I'm living with this man and I'm afraid of him. He threatens me and I know that we should not be living like this, living together." She didn't know what to do. Wanda wanted to leave but he threatened her; she was afraid for their little girls. She then asked me if she could go to church with me on Sunday, and I said, "Sure, I'll take you." I asked Wanda if she had ever received the baptism of the Holy Spirit, and she had not. She wanted to and asked if I could take her someplace to receive the baptism. I said yes and told Wanda that they taught it at my church. I took her up to the church, but as we sat there and listened, the pastor never mentioned the baptism of the Holy Spirit. When we left, Wanda was disappointed because she did not receive anything she thought could help her get her life together. "Well," I said, "I know another place where we could go." But when we arrived at Melody Land, it was closed, so we left. On the way home, God gently told me that I did not need to be dragging Wanda all over, that I could just pray with her. I asked God if she would receive it. It scared me, and I thought to myself, I don't know how to pray for her. But the Lord just said to pray with her. When we got home, we sat in the car and I asked Wanda if I could pray with her and she answered okay, so I started to pray with her. Then as I started praying in my heavenly language, Wanda just burst out and spoke in tongues. She was so happy and just so excited.

After I left and went home that night, I had a worrisome thought: Did she really receive that? God just reminded me to trust Him, that when He tells me to do something, I just have to obey. The next day Wanda came down to my corner and told me she was leaving and going back to New York. She was going home to pack her things and said that Raymond had not said anything about her leaving. Wanda asked me to pray that he wouldn't give her a hard time. I prayed for her. The next day she told me she had made a reservation. Wanda was leaving on Saturday and asked if I could take them to the airport. She was afraid of having Raymond take her. She said, "He'll make a fuss about it and I won't end up getting there." I was a little uncertain about doing this for her because I didn't want to get involved in their family affairs. So when I got home I prayed about it. I asked the Lord to show me what to do. When I went back on Friday, I told Wanda that I would take her to the airport. Saturday morning, I went and picked her up and she came down with all her clothes and her two little girls. She asked if Raymond could go with us. I told her yes, so we all got in the car and went up to the airport. Raymond didn't say a word the entire ride. Of course, at that time we could go up to the area where you boarded the planes. Raymond gave Wanda and the two little girls a kiss and then they got on the plane and left. I was a little bit nervous about going home with him because I didn't know what he was going to say or do; however, on the way home he was very quiet. I eventually spoke up and said, "Raymond, if you give your life to the Lord, God will put you back with Wanda and the two little girls. After all, they are your little girls. And if you get married, God will bless your family." His answer to me was that he wasn't ready for that yet. I let him know that I would be praying for him and Wanda, that God will lead him if he just sought Him. He thanked me and got out of the car. I went straight home.

During the summer, the Lord asked me to take a Bible to Raymond. I didn't know where to begin to find him since I had no idea if he was still living in the same place. However, I knew the Lord was leading me to reach out; I felt it so strongly in my spirit. I went to the Christian bookstore and bought a Bible, even though the Lord knew I didn't know where to find Raymond. I drove down the road for miles, clear to the end of Market Street, which was five miles long. I didn't see him anywhere, so I turned around and started back. "Lord, I'm doing the best I can, but I don't know where to find him." Then, all of a sudden, Raymond stepped out between two buildings. I pulled over to the curb and called him over. He came over to the car and I told him the Lord wanted me to bring him a Bible. He looked at me and said, "I've been praying that God would give me a Bible somehow." I said, "Well, here it is Raymond!" I encouraged him to read the Gospel of John, and he said he would. I reminded him that God could put him back with his family. All Raymond could do was thank me repeatedly. When I left I said, "Oh Lord, I just thank You. Sometimes I don't understand what You ask me to do but I want to obey even when I don't understand. You know what's taking place in all these lives that You put before me, so I thank You for Your concern for people and I just thank You that I am being obedient."

When I returned to my corner in the fall, I ran into Raymond's brother. His brother was still out here and I asked him how Raymond was doing. I asked him if Raymond was still here. His brother told me that Raymond had flown back to New York and that he and Wanda had married. Now, what if I had never talked to her? Obedience to God brings amazing results!

7

Discipline

God's Teaching

The ministry of Born Again Marriages was taking a different direction. This was the beginning of a new ministry. The Lord had instructed Marilyn Conrad, the overseer, to name it Covenant Keepers Inc., as God was a covenant keeper. Although we would no longer be able to meet at Lake Forrest, we began to meet weekly at Janeen's home in Irvine.

For a time, I attended by myself; but as time went on I started taking a couple of ladies with me. There we were not allowed to discuss our problems or our mates. At first, it was hard to not blurt out all that was going on and to not have our feelings get involved. Of course, getting into a big pity party was not allowed; instead, we worshiped the Lord and followed the teaching of the Word. If we were hurting, we could ask for prayer and they would lay hands on us in prayer. I always came home after feeling uplifted and confident in God. I also started attending some meetings in Pasadena at a couple's home who had a restored marriage, and what an encouragement they were.

Every day the Lord was working in my life and in my job. By this time, my job had been extended to seven and a half hours, and in that, God was teaching me to tithe to my church and supply food to the church to help those in need at Thanksgiving and Christmas. I joined the prayer chain at my church. God began to work, helping me to be obedient to Him, knowing that I needed the help and the guidance.

The enemy was always ready to set his trap. This time by tempting me with a certain man who had started to show affection toward me. At first, he just talked with me; then he would bring me flowers or an ice cream. Then he started to beg me to have dinner with him. I would tell him no, that I couldn't since I was married. I never did tell him we were separated, but he didn't see anything wrong with our going out for dinner. I kept refusing but his admiration for me and his gifts were working on my flesh. I started looking forward to him coming with all his kind words, and I broke down and gave him my phone number: wrong! He started calling me every night and asking me why we couldn't have dinner together.

Finally, one night God told me to get rid of him. I had almost let it go too far already, so the Lord was firm. God knew that my flesh was becoming weak and it was time to end this. God got me back on His level and what He was calling me to do concerning my marriage. One night when this man called, I had to swallow hard because I told him not to call me anymore and that I could not go out to dinner with him. There was silence on the other end of the phone and I was very frightened at what was going on in his mind. I just prayed. He begged me again and I told him again not to call because I could not go out for dinner and that if he called again I would not answer the phone. There was silence on the other end of the phone and then I just hung up. I prayed to God and asked Him to not let that man come back to my corner again and to not allow him to call me again. But he called again. The last time he called me, I didn't answer the phone and it finally ended.

I struggled with that for a few days because I felt bad about the whole thing, but I knew that I had to obey God. God knew what was going on.

Then one day God got my attention again. I came home from work and sat down on my recliner chair. I thought to myself, This chair is in bad shape and looks worn out. I thought about getting rid of Howard's chair and buying a different one. Then the Lord spoke to me and for some reason asked me to buy two chairs instead of one. I thought that was foolish. Why would I buy two chairs as there was no sign of my husband coming home. Howard was barely talking to me at that time. But I heard it again: buy two chairs instead of one. Still I struggled with that thought. Then I thought, Well, God has asked me to do strange things before. I will do what He says and believe that God is guiding me. God reminded me to walk by faith and not by sight, asking that I now put my faith into action! I knew that God was speaking to me and I bought two matching chairs.

One day I came home from work and started flipping through a catalog, just looking at some clothes, and I came across this really pretty dress. I thought about how this would be nice when we renewed our vows, and I felt the Lord ask me to order it and hang it in my closet. As I sat there, I thought to myself, Oh, here we go again. There was no sign that Howard was ever coming home. Once again, the Lord reminded me that "substance is the things hoped for and evidence of things not seen," so I ordered the dress. I hung it in my closet where it continued to hang for a number of years after. I also never hung any of my clothes on Howard's side of the closet. His side of the closet remained empty while he was gone. The Lord just told me to expect Howard to bring his clothes back and put them in that space, so I believed.

Later, Howard started calling me a little more and came down several times. It started to seem like he wanted to come home. Then suddenly during his visits, he'd just say he had to leave. I didn't really know what was going on in his mind but I had a feeling that things were not going well with this other woman. Then at Easter time, the Lord told me to take a card and a chocolate Easter egg up to him at his apartment. I thought, I can't do that; the other woman might be there. Oh Lord, if this is You, make me understand why You're telling me to do this. That just doesn't make any sense to me. But as the days went by, I felt that word just overwhelm me and pursue my thoughts. Finally, I said, "Okay, Lord, I will, but I really think it's a bad idea." I got a card and a chocolate Easter egg, not knowing at all even how to get to Howard's place. I was scared, but I tell you, the Lord just led me all the way. I was amazed at how I drove right up to his apartment. Once I arrived, I was too afraid to go up, but I prayed and asked the Lord to remove this fear from me. I said, "I will trust that You are with me." I went up to the door and rang the bell, but no one answered. I was pretty relieved. I decided to leave the card and egg by his door. The next day he called me and said that he would stop by. Everything God has asked me to do always connects with His plan. About this time, I became aware that Howard was no longer visiting the woman in Arizona. I believed God was moving in his life and I felt more confident that Howard would soon decide to come back home.

After that I did not hear from Howard for a long time. I called his apartment and he was no longer there; his phone had been disconnected. I was worried and wondered what could have happened. I just finally prayed and prayed and committed the situation to God. I wanted to panic but God intervened every time and took my attention back to His Word. He would show me how I was giving in to fear and doubts, that I needed to resist Satan's tools again. Finally, after several weeks, I received a call from Howard. He told me he had moved in with another trucker to share expenses. I believed him that it was another trucker, only to find out it was another woman, which shattered my faith for a while.

However, God was not going to let me drop my role of standing for my marriage and I continued to hold onto His promises. I felt so devastated but He reminded me of Jonah and how Jonah felt in the belly of the whale:

I descended to the roots of the mountains. The earth with its bars was around me forever, but You have brought up my life from the pit, O LORD my God. While I was fainting away, I remembered the LORD, and my prayer came to You, into Your holy temple. Those who regard vain idols forsake their faithfulness, but I will sacrifice to You with the voice of thanksgiving. That which I have vowed I will pay. Salvation is from the LORD. (Jonah 2:6-9)

In other words, God was telling me through His Word that I was listening to lying vanities just like Jonah was while in the belly of the whale, and that I was forgetting His faithfulness. I knew that God had been speaking to me through His Word and that He was still going to fulfill His word. How? That was where my faith in Him had to be. God continued to show me how to walk in His love at my job, to pray, and to fast, for it always strengthened my faith.

God was working in my life for there was a ministry up the street from my corner called His Nesting Place. This was a place where they took in young girls that had gotten in trouble or were pregnant. The ministry would house them and help them deliver their babies. Some of the young girls would come down to my corner and talk with me, and I'd share Christ's love for them. Some would ask if they could go to church with me. I always said yes. On Wednesdays, I would pick them up and take them to church at Calvary Chapel Downey. They were getting ministered to at His Nesting Place as well, but once in a while they enjoyed going to church with me; their leaders were happy to let me take them along. God just kept me busy for Him while I kept praying for my husband and my family as well.

God still had some cleaning up to do in my life. As I said in the beginning, I did not like the lifestyles of Howard's family. I did not agree with their language, dirty stories, smoking, and drinking, which made me take a dislike to them. I knew in my heart that was wrong but I didn't know how to respond as the Bible says to. I never said anything to them but would voice my opinion to my husband, to which he would reply, "Well, I can't do anything about that." I continued to carry this anger and attitude, especially when I would have them over and we would get together. When our separation happened, the Lord asked me to go to them and ask for forgiveness.

I didn't know how, for it meant that I would have to reveal how I felt toward them. Oh, God I can't do that. The Holy Spirit convicted me. I don't know how to explain it but I just couldn't get any rest. Finally, I consented, thinking, Oh Lord, I will, but I'm scared. They probably will comment, "Oh, so now you want to ask for forgiveness" and I am afraid of their reactions. But I knew I had to do it; it was God's mandate in my life. So I got in the car and headed to my brother-in-law's place, who is married to my niece. At this time, he had a real alcohol problem, which was about to break up their marriage; but on my way to their place, I got cold feet and decided to stop at my sister's place, thinking maybe I could forget about it.

When I got to their place, they were getting ready to go to the airport to pick up a family member, so I had to leave anyway. My niece and her husband lived only a few miles from my sister, and the Lord said not to turn back now. When I got to their place, Don came out of the house with a can of beer in his hand. We never showed any kind of love toward one another, and he just said, "Sylvia is in the house; go on in." I went in and she offered me a cup of coffee. She poured me a cup and I sat at the end of the table. I had barely sat down when Don walked in the door. I really didn't have time to think before the Holy Spirit took over, and I got up and walked up to Don. I explained that I was there for one reason: to ask for his forgiveness for the kind of sister-in-law I had been. His reaction shocked me. He told me that he should be the one asking for forgiveness. I explained again that God had sent me to apologize and ask for forgiveness. Don told me that he had always felt that I was a good Christian. I was ashamed and explained that I was still learning how to be a good Christian. He cried and I cried and we both hugged each other. To this day we have a healed relationship.

After that, Don was able to get help for his problem. He talked to the pastor of the Lutheran Church they were attending and the pastor helped him a lot. Today, he is totally delivered from the alcohol problem and is active in their church.

Later I went to my other brother-in-law and his wife and I did the same thing. They didn't understand my inner heart since they thought I was a good Christian, until I explained my heart attitude. After Howard returned home, Ron's wife, Shirley, got very ill with cancer and she wanted only me to take her for her treatments. She prayed with me to receive Jesus into her life.

God changed our lives and brought healing and restoration. Even today Howard's youngest sister, her husband, and all their children are saved and active church members. His older sister and I have a wonderful relationship also.

8

Guidance

God's Protection

O ne day, I crossed a mother and three of her daughters. She started to share her problems with me. Her husband was in the United States illegally. He didn't have his U.S. citizenship and was on drugs. She asked me to pray. As we got to know each other, sometimes I would go to her home and we would pray together for her husband. She was a good mother to her children. Sometimes he would leave for several days and she would ask to pray with me. Finally, one day he came to me and started asking questions about what I was saying to his wife. He explained that she was always talking about God and Jesus. I shared the Word with him and asked him if he wanted to turn his life over to the Lord. If he did, God would help him get his life in the right direction. He just shook his head and told me he wasn't ready to do that, so his wife and I continued to pray for him. One evening she called me and was crying because he hadn't come home; she wanted to go look for him.

I had to tell her no. I explained that she shouldn't go out there alone but that we should pray. As soon as I hung up, my phone rang again and it was her husband. He had come home and wanted to talk about the Lord. He asked who this Jesus was we kept talking about. I told him what He did for us because He loved us so much. I shared the Word and he said I sounded so convincing. I asked if he would pray with me and ask Jesus Christ to come into his life. He said, "Yes, I'm convinced by your confidence." We then prayed and I told him to take his wife to church where they could get grounded. She told me that he was around more and said that he drove away from the crowd that he had been hanging around with.

A few weeks later, one of the guys he had been hanging around with stole his motorcycle. Ernie found out who had it and went to their home to get it. Sharon told him not to go but he was angry and he wanted to get it back. He knocked on the door and when they opened it he told the guy he came to get his bike. They pulled a knife on him. He managed to get away, ran behind the house, jumped the fence and through some other backyards. Meanwhile they called the police. The police drove around the block, saw him running, and flashed the spotlight on him. They called over the loudspeaker for him to stop but he didn't and they shot and killed him.

I was shocked when Sharon called and told me. When I went to church on Sunday morning, I prayed, "Lord, he just accepted You. Why didn't You protect him?" I was in tears when I walked into church. I shared it with one of the ushers and he reminded me that I needed to praise the Lord, that Ernie was in heaven now. I put my trust in God's plan for this family. I spent a lot of time with the family through that difficult time. At the time of his death, she had five children, and the youngest was just a baby.

Another mother I crossed had four boys. At the time she was living with a man but she was unhappy and shared her grief with me. God was able to give me such boldness. I told her that God couldn't bless a relationship like that and explained that if she got out of that relationship God would bring the right person into her life, then she would be in God's will. She told him to leave and he came to talk to me. He seemed like a nice fellow but he didn't take to her boys as a father figure, so it continually bothered her. I shared the Lord with him and I apologized for how things were working out for him. I told him that God loved him and had a plan for his life as well, and then I prayed for him. He ended up moving out.

The two youngest boys, Frankie and Andy, wanted to go to church with me, so I would pick them up every Sunday morning and take them to their Sunday school class at Calvary. One Sunday when we came home, the oldest one said, "Lorraine, I had a dream about you last night." I responded, "I hope it was a good one." He said, "Yes, I dreamed you had a mansion in heaven." All I responded with was "Good, I receive that." They went with me every Sunday morning, and then their mother and the oldest boy went with me to church a few times until they all moved away.

I had a lot of praying to do when I got home from work and every day I would start my day with my confession. One morning as I arrived on my corner and I began crossing the children, I noticed there was a car parked across the street on Market with a man just sitting in the car. When I got out into the middle of the street to cross the children, he just motioned to me with his finger to approach the car. Well, I didn't know who he was, so I crossed the children and went back to get another group of children who were waiting. When I got to the middle of the street, I looked over and he motioned again. I was very concerned but I did go closer to the car and he asked me to go around to the other side. I was very scared as he was pretty adamant about it, but when I bent over to look at him he flashed his badge at me explaining he was an undercover agent. The SWAT team was coming out to the area to break up a big drug ring behind the liquor store. He asked me to keep the children out of the way. I asked him to explain how I could do that; I had a bunch of children. His response was to just do it.

When I started back across the street, the truck with the SWAT team pulled up. Eight men jumped out and some took positions in the street, down on their knees, pointing their guns at the liquor store. Some got up on the roof, pointing their guns down. I cried out, "Oh Lord! Help me keep the children safe!" I motioned to some children across the street to stand still and I kept all the children by me up against the building. Fortunately, the gang members all surrendered without firing any guns. All I could do was just thank the Lord. Some parents were driving their children to school and they told the principal what was happening on the corner. He came out and over to my corner and asked if I needed help but it was all over by then. My supervisor came out later as the principal had called and told her what had happened and asked why she hadn't sent some help up to me. But the undercover agents did not inform them in case it would leak out and the bunch would get wind of it. My supervisor was very upset about it since they didn't inform them of the incident. The city then decided we needed to carry phones on our belts as we had no way of getting in touch with them if we needed help. Sometimes I would be exhausted when I got home, but the Lord reminded me that He was the strength of my life.

Every day a certain little boy would catch the bus to school, but one day he missed it. Not only was it raining, but he was soaking wet, his parents were at work, and the doors were locked. I told him I would drive him to school but he had to wait until I had my break time since I couldn't leave my corner. Later another little boy arrived late and missed the bus too. Before I knew it, I was driving both of them to school. I was later called into my supervisor's office. She asked me if I had driven the boys and I said yes.

I was asked never to do that because if anything were to happen, the city could get sued. I felt very sorry for what I had done but she knew that I meant well and that I was a good crossing guard but that I just needed to be careful about some things. She suggested that the next time something similar happened, just to send them to school and the school would see that they got to their regular places. I went home thanking the Lord once again for helping me through that situation.

One day a group of children were coming home from school; they were arguing and fighting. I helped them across the street and they went into the liquor store and were really getting into it. They came out of the liquor store and then back on my side, and they were pushing and shoving and calling each other names. I then remembered the Christian tracts I had in my pocket and I said, "Here, kids, I have something for you." I handed each one a tract. They looked at it and then they looked at me and soon turned and went their separate ways with no more action. Later I crossed a little girl who asked me if there was a fight on that corner and I told her no. She said that they were planning on it when they left school. I looked at her and said, "The Lord prevented it."

9

Chaos

God's Watchful Eye

By this time, I started having trouble with the Cadillac. It had a short somewhere in the electrical system and it kept running my battery down. I had to call AAA to come out and jump-start it for me to get to work and sometimes even to get home. Sometimes I'd have to find someone who had cables to start it for me. I had been taking a few kids to the Wednesday evening youth group at Calvary. One day after I picked the last girl up, I stopped at a red light and my car stopped. I was hoping it would start but it didn't. I kept trying, but it just wouldn't start. Then one of the girls said, "Lorraine, you pray about everything, Why don't you pray and ask God to start it?" Boy, was I humiliated or what! I answered, "You're right." I sat and prayed and thanked God that He allowed us to get to church and back. I turn the ignition on and it started and they all shouted. We went to church and I got them all home.

However, it kept getting worse. I was told of places to take it and have it checked. It cost me lots of money for them to just check it out but no one could find the short. AAA started charging me because they had to come out every so often to start my car. I began praying and thanking God for a new car, one I wouldn't have to worry about: Thank You, Lord, that You are the source of all my needs. I for some reason asked specifically for a red car, not knowing why.

Howard happened to call one night. He just wanted to see how I was doing. I told him about my car situation and he said he'd give me $800 for a car but that was all. He said that he knew some guy who had a car that didn't have too many miles on it. Howard said that he would talk to him and call me to take me to see the car. I asked Howard if he would mind if I went looking also. He said to go ahead, that he'd call in a few days. I read an ad from a car dealership in Anaheim, so I thought maybe I'd run out there and take a look at the cars. I was looking at the cars that they had marked down and I saw this little red Mini Plymouth Van. I thought what a prayer closet my car would be. It was priced at $18,000  but with a markdown of $1,000, which then was $17,000. The salesman said that if I bought it that weekend, they would come down another $1,000, making it $16,000. My friend Rod was working across from this dealership and asked me to call him when I went looking if I needed a man with me when dealing with cars. So I called him and he came over to talk with the salesperson. I told the salesman that I needed to check with my husband. He said that they would hold it until after the weekend. Rod walked me to my car and we prayed. He prayed for Howard, my conversation with him, and that God would go before me. That night I was kind of nervous as Satan was trying to put fear in me, but I kept resisting it. Since Howard had informed me he would give me $800 for a car, Satan was trying to get me to relinquish telling Howard about it.

When he called a day later, I did panic a little but he asked what I found out or if I had come across a deal. It was like the Holy Spirit took over my mouth. I told him the deal and that if I bought it that weekend they would knock off another $1,000 and the final cost would be $16,000. He never hesitated and said, "Go buy it. I will get the money to you." I then realized that God was involved in this conversation and that He truly did go before me. My new car became my prayer closet during my break times. I also took several young people to Wednesday evening youth ministry at Calvary. God honored me even in my anxious times and in my fears, but it was not my feelings but my trust in God and my faith in His Word.

Rod and his wife, Marietta, met with me at a meeting they were having and they all laid hands on my car and prayed that God would use this for His purpose. These are the scriptures that the Lord showed me:

This I recall to my mind, therefore I have hope. The LORD'S loving kindnesses indeed never cease, for His compassions never fail. They are new every morning; great is Your faithfulness. "The LORD is my portion," says my soul, "Therefore I have hope in Him." The LORD is good to those who wait for Him, to the person who seeks Him. It is good that he waits silently for the salvation of the LORD. (Lamentations 3:21-26)

I felt God talking to me through this word!

The name of the LORD is a strong tower; The righteous runs into it and is safe. (Proverbs 18:10)

Obey God even if you are not quite sure how it will turn out. In 1 Samuel 15:22, God teaches us that obedience is better than sacrifice. God was telling me that He wanted my obedience more than my sacrifice and the pain and all that went with my stand for my marriage. The three young Hebrew men facing a fiery furnace said, "We know our God is able to deliver us and He will deliver us out of your hand, your majesty, but if he doesn't, please understand, sir, and even then, we will never under any circumstance serve your god." God was asking me through this situation if I was ready to take that kind of stand for my marriage, believing all so He can deliver my marriage from destruction and restore it. But if not, I would bow to the world's standards. I responded with, "I am. I put my faith and trust in You, Lord."

God was keeping me busy and in others' lives while He was working in my marriage. Sometimes when I went to bed I would just say, "Oh Lord, I'm falling into Your arms tonight and receiving Your peace and comfort so that I will be ready for another day."

Sometimes, we had heavy rains and the water would be so high on the curve that it would go down into my boots. I would carry the little ones past the curve so that they wouldn't get their feet wet. I always made sure I had all the cars stopped before I would help them across. I depended thoroughly on God's help and guidance. Still, I felt I needed a better job so that I could make more money. I wanted to prove to Howard that I could do better and bring in more money.

There were openings for a couple of jobs in Long Beach that paid better and I thought they would be good. I had to take a test for each one but someone told me that as long as you worked for the city they would pick city workers first, so I was pretty happy about that. I later took one test, passed the test, but was informed that they had filled the position. I felt so disappointed, but I tried the next job. I took the test, passed, and later got the same report. I was pretty upset and wondered why I didn't get one of those jobs. It bothered me for some time. Then God revealed to me that I had the wrong attitude in that I did not have to get another job to prove anything to Howard. God would supply my needs in every way and use me as I walked with Him.

I began to have leaks in two places in my house during the rainy season. Yes, that meant I needed to put a new roof on my house. I told God that I needed to do something else, that I couldn't afford all that. Someone told me that maybe I could get part-time work at the arena in downtown Long Beach as a hostess; the pay was pretty good but it would mean evening work. Most of the time I only had to work one shift and I would be home by 10 o'clock; but there were a few times I would have to work a double shift because someone didn't show up or was sick. The Lord had opened that door for me and He was my strength. The only time I didn't like it was when they had the rock concerts, but God would remind me to just pray for the young people. I would pray wherever I was stationed. I saw things I couldn't believe. I witnessed to some young people when God would make it possible for me to do. I was able to get the roof done on my house, all praise to God.

Behold, how happy is the man whom God reproves, so do not despise the discipline of the Almighty. For He inflicts pain, and gives relief; He wounds, and His hands also heal. From six troubles He will deliver you, even in seven evil will not touch you. (Job 5:17-19)

This also comes from the LORD of hosts, Who has made His counsel wonderful and His wisdom great. (Isaiah 28:29)

By this time, Ron and Debbie were married and they were living in Camarillo, California. They would invite me to spend Christmas, Thanksgiving, or the holidays with them. One year, Debbie baked a lot of Christmas cookies and I asked her why she was baking so many. She simply replied that she just wanted to bake a bunch of Christmas cookies. She asked if I would help her decorate them and I said sure. We worked at that all while she was also baking other things. I kind of wondered at all that she was doing, but I guess she just wanted to bake. Then, the next morning, Debbie said we would go get groceries and bring them home. Next, we would go pick up the dogs, which had been taken to be bathed and groomed. After getting the groceries, we were heading home and I was unaware of where we were. I didn't know my way around up there, and we wound up at the dog place instead. I thought we were going to take the groceries home first, but Debbie thought that we'd go ahead and get the dogs first. Because I didn't know my way around, I hadn't realized that, after buying the groceries and heading home, Debbie had seen Ron's van in the driveway. So she drove away from the house to the dog groomers to give him time to do what they had planned. When we walked in the door, I saw two great big boxes in the living room all Christmas wrapped and Ron was sitting on the couch. They had gotten in touch with Howard and had told him to come over for Christmas. This is while he was with the woman in Arizona. When I walked in, Ron and Debbie said, "Open your boxes." I said, "For heaven sake, what in the world did you get me?" I couldn't even imagine what it could be, so I started to tear off the paper of the first box. It burst open and a young man was inside. I was so startled as I didn't know who he was. My son asked why I didn't recognize him? I was just stunned. He had a beard and I had never seen him with a beard before. Then I tore

the second paper and it burst open. There was Sue, my daughter-in-law, and my granddaughter, Sarah (around six years old). What a surprise!

Howard showed up for Christmas but broke down and cried. Of course he blamed me for all that happened. Yes, some of it was true. I hadn't been the wife that I should have been, but I had to overlook his faults too. I don't remember if Howard stayed overnight or if he left later. I thanked the kids for what they had done for me and later on I returned home. After a few days off for Christmas vacation, it was time to return to work.

It was some time before I had any contact with Howard, but one morning as I was getting ready to go to work, the doorbell rang and a policeman stood at the door. He handed me some papers and told me I was served with divorce papers and advised me to get myself an attorney.

I was shocked. When I closed the door, I started to cry and asked the Lord how He could let this happen. I had been standing and praying. Through the Holy Spirit, God asked me if I was going to let the devil have this marriage, or was I going to take my stand? I threw the papers on the floor and stomped all over them. I cried out, "Devil, you will not have this marriage! It is in God's hands."

10

Miracles

God's Promises Fulfilled

The Lord spoke to my heart not to get an attorney, but I got an attorney in disobedience to God at the urging of my children. They did not understand my stand. I prayed for a Christian attorney and one was referred to me as a very good attorney. During these court proceedings, I was constantly seeking God. He gave me a word that I wrote down and placed in a little Bible I carried with me any time I had to go to court: "Fear not the size of your problem." I found further encouragement in this verse:

> He shall say to them, "Hear, O Israel, you are approaching the battle against your enemies today. Do not be fainthearted. Do not be afraid, or panic, or tremble before them, for the LORD your God is the one who goes with you, to fight for you against your enemies, to save you." (Deuteronomy 20:3-4)

Then I wrote, "Today I will approach this battle against the Devil and his forces. I refuse to be fainthearted and fearful, and I will not tremble. I will not be terrified at the sight of my enemy: the other woman. Remember the Lord."

I shared with Janeen about the attorney I had who was supposedly a Christian. She too hired him and she thought at that time he was doing okay.

This attorney set a court date and then called to tell me that it had been canceled because his computer had broken down and that we had to set another date. However, later he sent a bill for the court appointment that we had never had. I called and asked him why he charged me for that court date. My daughter called the attorney and was very angry with him because he charged me for that. He was upset with my daughter but called and offered to split the cost.

When we went to court to go before the judge, my lawyer stood up and asked for a recess as he wanted to speak to Howard and me. We walked out of the courtroom and into a private room. During that meeting, Howard said that he would continue to pay for the house for five years but after that he would sell the house and all the proceeds would be his. After this meeting, it was too late to go back to court so our case was canceled, resulting in another huge bill. It turned out that my attorney was unnecessarily charging me for things: unnecessary meetings, calls, and so forth. This was costing so much money that I was starting to panic.

I shared these things with my friend Janeen, who had used him as an attorney in the past. She prayed with me, we talked, and she urged me to continue, that the attorney was just trying to help. The Lord told me to get rid of that attorney. Fear overwhelmed me but I wasn't going to let fear control me. I called the attorney and told him I no longer needed his services. He was angry and told me I wouldn't have anyone to support me. I reminded him I had God. The case was eventually dropped completely. I then called Howard and told him that I would sign the papers. So he came over and brought the papers with him. Howard did not have an attorney, so he completed and submitted the divorce papers and had them processed on his own. I just signed the papers.

After that the lawyer turned around and tried to take advantage of Janeen. He was trying to take all of the money that she was supposed to receive. Janeen's husband stepped in and they reported what the attorney was doing and found out that he was taking advantage of women. The truth came out about all that he was doing and he was disbarred. God told me to get rid of that attorney.

I was encouraged by the Holy Spirit through His Word to do a Jericho march around our house. Every morning I would get ready for work and I would walk around my house. For six days I walked around the house every morning. On the seventh day, I marched around the house seven times and then I praised the Lord. The house now, first and foremost, belonged to God, then to Howard and me, as it should have been.

Howard married again in 1988 but that marriage only lasted six years. During the time Howard was married to that woman, he came and told me that he knew he had made a big mistake, but that it was too late; there was too much water under the bridge, and he didn't think there was a way out. When he left, once again I realized I needed to take authority against the lies and deception of the enemy, which I did.

I was now able to apply for Social Security, so I went to sign up but found out it was necessary to get a copy of the divorce papers. I went to the courthouse in Pasadena on my break time from my job to get my papers. There was a long line and I knew I didn't have enough time because I needed to get back to work. As I stood there, a lady came up to me in the line and asked me what I was there for. I told her that I was there to get my divorce papers. She took me up to the window and told the man at the front to get my divorce papers and she left. I looked at the line of people standing there, wondering what they might have thought since she pulled me out of the line and took me up to the window at the front. When I turned to thank her, she was nowhere to be found. I was encouraged once again, knowing that God was watching over me.

They brought the papers up and the attorney went through all of them, one at a time. Then he looked up at me and he said, "You are not divorced. These papers weren't completed correctly. You had better get yourself an attorney."

However, the Lord said to me, "Don't tell anyone." As I headed back to work, I praised the Lord all the way, for I knew that He was with me.

I was back on my job again and this is when God asked me to go up and see Howard at his work. I thought, God, You have to be kidding. He's married and You want me to go up and see him? That didn't sound reasonable to me, so I just tried to push the thought off and go back to work. But I couldn't get rid of the thought; it kept coming to me day after day. I just kept thinking, How foolish! I mean, I don't see any connection with doing this, but it continued to be so strong. Finally, one day when I came home from work, I just said, "Okay, Lord, I will do it. Even though I don't understand this. I will obey." I started out but I only got maybe a mile or two down the road and just couldn't do it. I turned around and went home. I was upset with myself because I knew I felt the strong urging of God to do this, so I started out again. I was driving down the freeway, and every time there was a turn-off, I would debate whether to get off; but somehow, I couldn't get off the freeway. The whole way, I struggled with the desire to turn around, but I kept going and I finally arrived at the warehouse.

I pulled up to the security guard's shack. I walked up to the security guard, trembling, and asked him if

Howard had come in yet. He answered, "Yes, I believe he has, but they don't pull in at this place anymore. The trucks pull in a block down the street." He told me to just go down the street and I would see it. Then he asked me to just wait a minute so that he could call and make sure Howard was there. My heart just dropped when I heard that Howard was in. I got in my car and I drove down. I didn't even see them because I was so nervous. I went around the block and when I came to the warehouse and was pulling up on the corner, Howard's truck came in. He waved at me and pointed to tell me where to park and I then pulled over and parked. He got out of the truck and jumped in the car with me and the first thing he tried to do was give me a kiss. "Oh," I said, as I moved back in my seat, "well, no, I have just been thinking a lot about you and wondered how you were. I just thought I would come up to see you." He was very tickled that I actually came up to see him. He told me he was so glad to see me; we ended up talking for a long time and actually had a very good conversation. Then, as I got ready to leave, he said, "I'll be down to see you in a few days." On my drive home, the Lord reminded me how "what seems foolish to man is the wisdom of God," and that through me obeying in going to see Howard, he realized that I hadn't rejected him. I just cried and praised the Lord, because He knows everything, and if we just obey His plan, everything will work out for our good.

During my sixteenth year on the corner of Market and Locust, I decided to retire. Of course, God was still in control of my life in His own loving way. As the last week of school approached, I put in for my retirement. One day, as I was coming around the corner of my street, I saw some children and mothers standing on my corner. I wondered why they were already on the corner, but when I got close to where I parked, I saw a huge sign on the side of the building. The children had cut out the letters and pasted them on a huge banner with the words "We love our Crossing Guard Lorraine Woodhouse," with balloons tied to the light  post on my corner. When I got out of my car, the mothers said they were going to kidnap me and take me over to the school for opening exercises. They told me not to be concerned as they had already called my supervisor and informed her and that she was sending a substitute for the time that I would be gone.

When I got to the school, they had a grocery cart all decorated with a sign around it: "We love our Crossing Guard." I received a bouquet of flowers and a plaque from the city. Then the social worker of the school took me to each classroom. One child in each classroom had been appointed the spokesperson for that class and handed me a folder full of notes that the children had written to me. I was so overwhelmed and humbled. I had no idea that I was to be honored in such a way. God was continuing to prove to me that He had done all this work in my life. I really did not know how to respond. All I could do was just accept their hospitality and love.

Before the last day of school, my supervisor came out to my corner and urged me to put in a bid for another corner and stay on as a crossing guard, and I consented. God knew I needed to continue to work and was still going ahead of me. I put my bid in on another corner in a very nice area. My hours were cut to six and a half hours and I was still in a crossing area with no signal light, but I started the new job the next year on Stearns and Charlemagne. I continued to pass out stickers, pencils, and tracts for the children of this corner. I was happy there because it was a quieter area.

I would sit on my chair by a lady's house as I waited for the children to come. I did have a very close call on this corner. One day a young driver swung around the stopped cars and ran the stop sign. I had just stepped off the curb to move into the middle of the street to bring the children across, and the driver missed me by a breath. I knew that God was my helper always.

When I started my job at this new intersection, I was informed that the other crossing guard would let some of the children play on the playground until it was time for her to leave. She would go over to the school and gather those who needed to cross with her before she left. I was sure I could do that, so I did. Every day when it was time for me to leave, I would go over to the school and gather the children and bring them across the street before I went home. One day when I went over to pick up the children after school, I came around the corner just as the principal of the school came out; she said she needed to talk to me. She told the children to go down to the crosswalk and wait until I came over. They looked at me and then at the principal with a look of apprehension. After they left, she asked me if I was passing out Christian tracts and things to the children. I was frightened but I admitted that I did. She told me, "Quit it! You are not allowed to pass religious things out on the school property. I will turn you in if you don't stop." I just agreed. She turned and left and I went down to the children to cross them. Of course, they were curious about what was wrong. I just said she had some instructions for me. The children then started asking me for those tracts and stickers that I had been giving them. I told them the principal of the school said I was not allowed to give them out anymore. Some of the parents came to me and told me not to let her stop me and that I was not on school property. They asked me to keep passing them out, that the children loved them. "Don't let her scare you. We will defend you," they encouraged me. I was ashamed that I let fear stop me, but then God stepped in. The next year the principal from

the school on Market and Locust was transferred to Sterns and Charlemagne, the corner that I was on. She found out that I was the crossing guard there and she was so pleased because she knew how the children at Jane Adams liked me. God showed me in so many ways that His leading, His guidance, and His discipline were in my life.

Howard and Galen took a fishing trip to Canada and flew out of Ontario airport. Howard decided to leave his car at the airport and upon his return had an unpleasant experience. When he opened his car door, all his clothes were in the back seat with a note from his non-covenant wife: "Don't come back!" So Howard moved in with his sister Dorothy. For Christmas of 1996, our children decided to come

to California for the holidays to be with me. Howard's sister invited them over for Christmas dinner but did not extend an invitation to me. Howard had stopped by to see me on his way home from work and invited me to the dinner. He said he would come by and pick me up.

He stayed very close to me during the entire visit, and all of his family was very nice to me and expressed that they were glad to see me.

In 1997, shortly after that get-together, Howard showed up at the back door of the house with his clothes. I was speechless. Howard stood there and said, "I'm coming home. We're going to work this out." We were not going to talk about what happened. I agreed, but I indicated that there would be no intimate relationship until we worked out the basics of our marriage.

On October 12, 1997, we renewed our vows in California in the presence of many friends and family. Rod and Marietta Cage, who also had a restored marriage and who both were now ordained ministers, were present and officiated at the ceremony. Our daughter sang "To God be the glory great things He has done" and I wore the dress I still had hanging in the closet after all those years.

Howard had been gone for 18 years but relationships with our various family members on both sides were restored. During those years, much prayer went in for all family members and many of them came to the knowledge of the Lord Jesus Christ.

Howard was happy to be home and I was happy he was home. I asked God to help me to be the wife that He had been teaching me to be, to revere, respect, honor, and obey him. I knew that it was up to the Lord to lead Howard to what church we would go to as a restored couple. Howard ended up asking me where I had been attending church and I told him Calvary Chapel; he never hesitated about attending Calvary and we both began to serve. After a few months of going there, he signed up to be an usher, and he attended the Men's Prayer Meetings every Saturday morning. Perhaps the devil is telling you that the person who you are interceding for will never change, that they are no good, but remember that they are another of God's chosen instruments, just like you.

Howard even came to the Covenant Keepers Annual Conference in Tulsa, Oklahoma, and there we renewed our vows once again with all of the Covenant Keepers present. Wouldn't you know, as the Lord would have it, it was the same day that the Covenant Keepers directors, Rex and Carolyn, renewed their vows at the same conference.

Howard and I both retired in 1999 after our renewal of vows in the fall. The next year in February, Howard gave me a beautiful Valentine card and told me I deserved a trip to Florida, and so we took a three-week road trip to Florida and went through many states.

It was even better than our first honeymoon, which was a lot shorter. One day after we got back, he told me he was going up to the store. When he came home, he handed me a little box. I looked at him a little puzzled but opened it. When I looked in the box, I found a beautiful golden angel bracelet. He hooked it on my wrist and said, "Angels are watching over you."

As time passed I had to make some changes in different areas concerning financial matters but I responded to God's teaching because Howard wanted to be in charge of all finances. He told me we needed to put our money together in the same bank and he would take care of the bills. That took me back a little and I had to get used to the idea of not being in control of the money anymore. God reminded me of my role as Howard's wife. There was such healing in both of us but I had also prayed fervently for God to work in Howard's life as well.

We got a mobile home in Ohio where we could spend a few months each year close to our children. It was just wonderful! I have no regrets for those difficult years because God did a beautiful work in both of our hearts and lives, even to the point of tithing—all miracles!

11

Howard's Final Destination

God's Blessing

The Lord called Howard home on April 1, 2005. We were blessed with over seven years of a restored marriage. During that time, we reaped the many benefits of God's hand in our lives as He rebuilt us into the two becoming one that was His plan all along. It was our hearts' desire that together in those years we would serve Him with zeal and excellence! We did just that, to God be the glory!

Made in the USA
Columbia, SC
04 June 2018